Best Editorial Cartoons of the Year

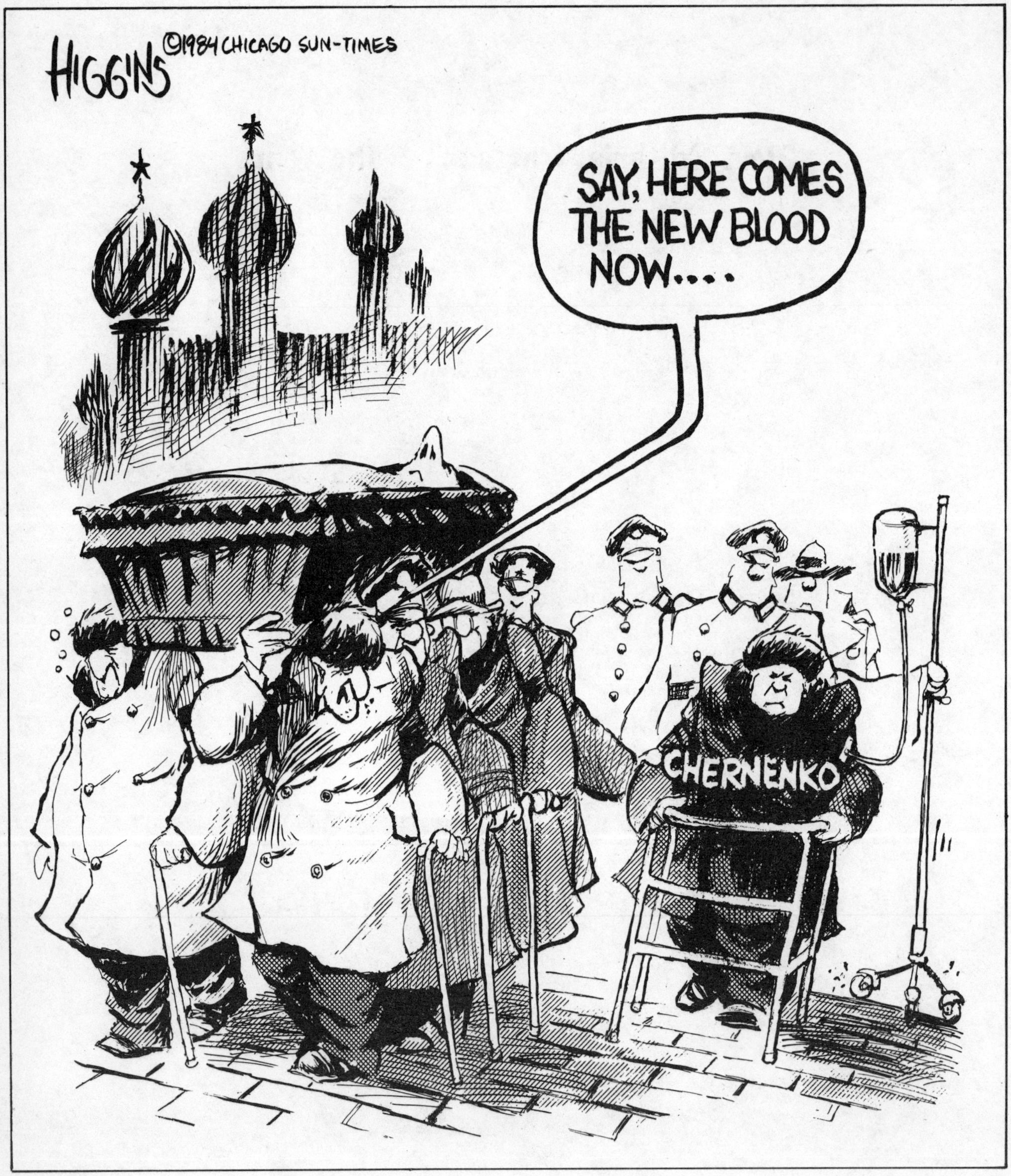
HIGGINS ©1984 CHICAGO SUN-TIMES
SAY, HERE COMES THE NEW BLOOD NOW....
CHERNENKO

JACK HIGGINS
Courtesy Chicago Sun–Times

BEST EDITORIAL CARTOONS OF THE YEAR

1985 EDITION

Edited by
CHARLES BROOKS

Foreword by **THOMAS P. "TIP" O'NEILL, JR.**

PELICAN PUBLISHING COMPANY
GRETNA 1985

I gratefully acknowledge the inestimable assistance of my granddaughter, Lisa Diane Hynds, in the preparation of this annual volume. She began as my assistant when she was barely ten years old—she's twenty now—and is efficiency personified.

Library of Congress Serial Catalog Data

Best editorial cartoons. 1972-
Gretna [La.] Pelican Pub. Co.
v. 29 cm. annual-
"A pictorial history of the year."

1. United States- Politics and government—
1969—Caricatures and Cartoons—Periodicals.
E839.5.B45   320.9'7309240207   73-643645
ISSN 0091-2220   MARC-S

Manufactured in the United States of America
Published by Pelican Publishing Company, Inc.
1101 Monroe Street, Gretna, Louisiana 70053

Contents

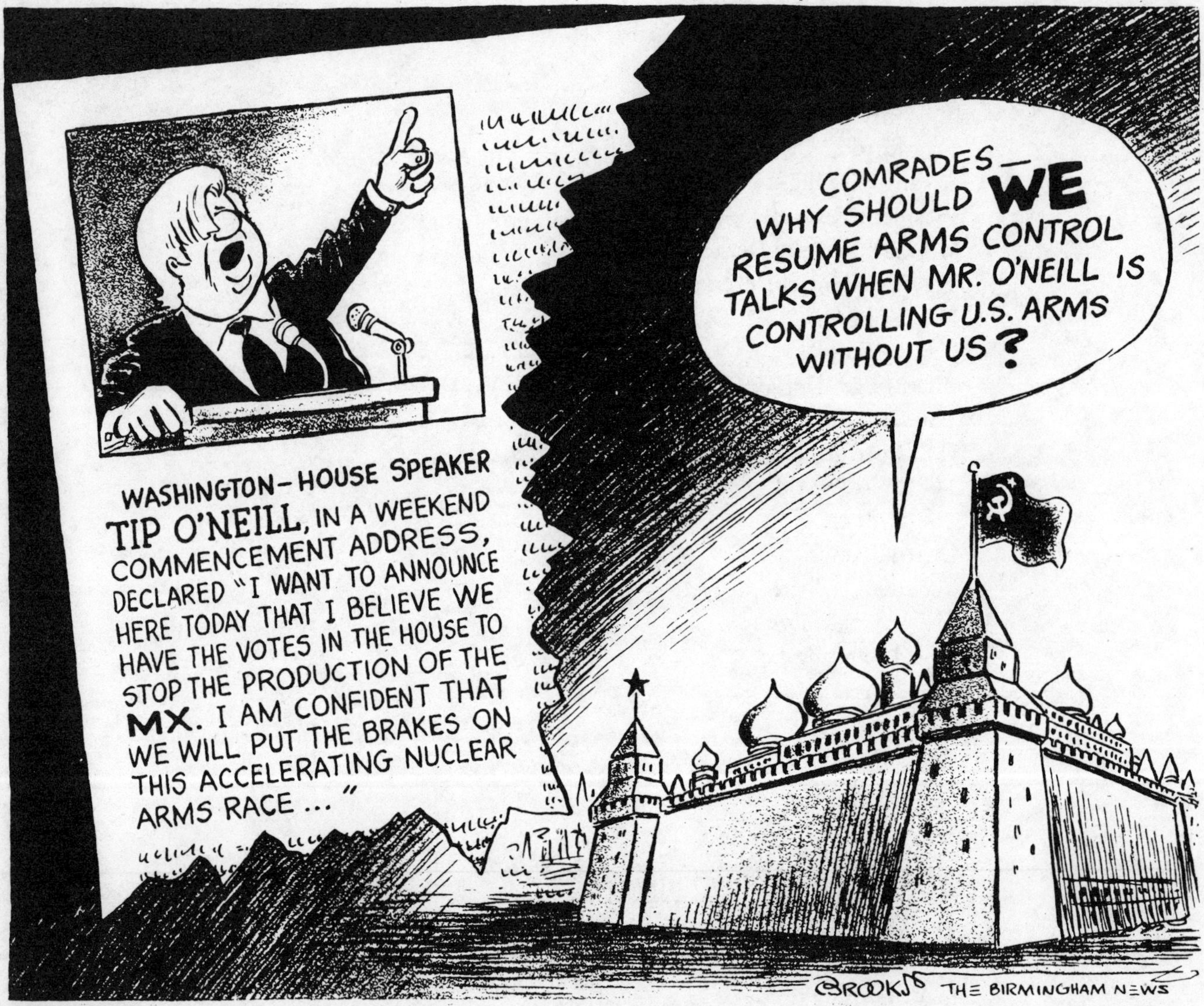
WASHINGTON–HOUSE SPEAKER TIP O'NEILL, IN A WEEKEND COMMENCEMENT ADDRESS, DECLARED "I WANT TO ANNOUNCE HERE TODAY THAT I BELIEVE WE HAVE THE VOTES IN THE HOUSE TO STOP THE PRODUCTION OF THE MX. I AM CONFIDENT THAT WE WILL PUT THE BRAKES ON THIS ACCELERATING NUCLEAR ARMS RACE ..."
COMRADES— WHY SHOULD WE RESUME ARMS CONTROL TALKS WHEN MR. O'NEILL IS CONTROLLING U.S. ARMS WITHOUT US?
BROOKS
THE BIRMINGHAM NEWS

CHUCK BROOKS
Courtesy Birmingham News

Foreword

MILT PRIGGEE
Courtesy Dayton Journal–Herald

Some people collect news clippings. I collect editorial cartoons. The walls of my Capitol office are covered with the brilliant works of Paul Szep and his many imaginative colleagues.

It has been said that a picture is worth a thousand words. That applies doubly to editorial cartoons. Not only do they reach more people, but they remain with us long after the printed word has been forgotten. A good sketch carries a wallop and leaves an impression that not even the best written editorial can match.

I speak from personal experience. Anyone who looks at the nation's editorial pages knows that I have been the target of some of our best cartoonists. I have been lauded and occasionally lampooned. Sometimes I have agreed with the point being made. Other times I have not. Sometimes I have laughed along with the cartoonist. Other times I have laughed even when it stings. I believe the walls of my Capitol office are testament to the fact that I have appreciated the humor even when I have not appreciated the point.

The fact is, it is impossible to ignore a good editorial cartoon. Artists who practice this trade challenge the First Amendment and win with every stroke of their pen. People remember a well-sketched cartoon long after the best-written column has faded from memory. Political cartoonists break through barriers of language and distance that words alone cannot penetrate. They overcome barriers of politics and philosophy by communicating with a vast array of people—people who don't read editorials, but cannot resist the cartoons.

'Yipe, Yipe, Yipe. . . .'

EDDIE GERMANO
Courtesy Brockton Daily Enterprise

Through a half-century of public life, I have been both applauded and criticized. Early on in life, I learned that you cannot please everyone all of the time. With this thought in mind, I sympathize with

FOREWORD

DICK WRIGHT
© Scripps-Howard Newspapers

anyone who takes on public issues, and that includes political cartoonists. They use the world as their canvas. They help us see social and economic realities in bold and dramatic terms. They keep a watchful eye on how we deal with the problems that face the world, and how we sometimes fail to deal with them.

Throughout history, political cartoonists have provided a valuable check on the powerful. Through tough analysis, they prevent politicians from getting too powerful. Through humor they keep us, the politicians, from taking ourselves too seriously.

The art of political cartooning can take on many forms. There are the "shockers," who leave no room for compromise, and then there are the more subtle types. There are conservatives and a few liberals like me. There are some whose messages you simply cannot predict and they're the ones you have to watch out for!

I invite you to enjoy the 1985 edition of the *Best Editorial Cartoons of the Year.* Nowhere is there better debate than in the editorial cartoons that greet us every day. They offer a great testimonial to our freedom and love of democracy.

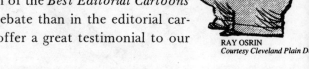

RAY OSRIN
Courtesy Cleveland Plain De

Speaker Thomas P. "Tip" O'Neill. Jr.
U.S. House of Representatives

BILL GARNER
Courtesy Washington Times

Award-Winning Cartoons

1984 OVERSEAS PRESS CLUB AWARD

DICK LOCHER
Editorial Cartoonist
Chicago Tribune

Born June 4, 1929, in Dubuque, Iowa; attended Loras College and the University of Iowa; former Air Force pilot and aircraft designer; studied art at the Chicago Academy of Fine Art and the Art Center of Los Angeles; assistant to Chester Gould, creator of the Dick Tracy comic strip, 1957-61; cartoonist for Dick Tracy comic strip, 1983 to present; editorial cartoonist for the *Chicago Tribune,* 1973 to present; winner of the Pulitzer Prize, 1983, the Sigma Delta Chi Award, 1982, and the Overseas Press Club Award, 1983; syndicated by the *Chicago Tribune.*

1983 SIGMA DELTA CHI AWARD
(Selected in 1984)

ROB LAWLOR
Editorial Cartoonist
Philadelphia Daily News

Former minor-league baseball player for farm clubs of the Los Angeles Dodgers, Kansas City Athletics, and St. Louis Cardinals; assistant in the art department of the *Philadelphia Daily News* at age eighteen, drawing theater and sports cartoons; editorial cartoonist, 1973 to present; singer, past guest on "The Mike Douglas Show"; professional dinner theater actor.

1984 NATIONAL HEADLINERS CLUB AWARD

STEVE BENSON
Editorial Cartoonist
Arizona Republic

Born in Sacramento, California, in 1953; reared in Dallas, Texas; cum laude graduate in political science, Brigham Young University, 1979; graduate, Art Instruction Schools, 1973; editorial cartoonist, *Arizona Republic,* 1980 to present; editorial cartoonist and research assistant, Republican Policy Committee, 1979-80; winner of Arizona Press Club Award for cartooning, 1980, 1981; formerly syndicated by the Washington Post Writers Group; presently syndicated by Tribune Media Services.

1984 THOMAS NAST AWARD

PAUL SZEP
Editorial Cartoonist
Boston Globe

Born in Hamilton, Ontario, Canada; graduate, Ontario College of Art, 1964; worked as a book and fashion illustrator and graphics designer; joined the *Boston Globe* in 1966 as an editorial cartoonist; won Pulitzer Prize, 1974 and 1977, Sigma Delta Chi Award, 1973 and 1976, and National Headliners Club Award, 1977.

1983 NATIONAL NEWSPAPER AWARD/CANADA
(Selected in 1984)

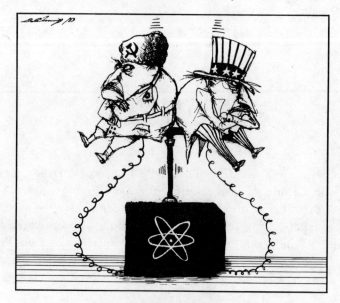

DALE CUMMINGS
Editorial Cartoonist
Winnipeg Free Press

Born in St. Thomas, Ontario, Canada; studied animation and illustration at Sheridan College; editorial cartoonist, *Winnipeg Free Press,* 1982 to present.

Best Editorial Cartoons of the Year

'I've just signed legislation outlawing the Democratic Party forever. Bombing starts November 6th!'

President Reagan

President Reagan continued to enjoy wide popularity during his fourth year in the presidency with the economy on the upswing, inflation under control, and unemployment down. His campaign for a second term was low-key from the start. Aside from a few appearances in key states and two televised debates with Walter Mondale, he kept close to the White House. The result: Reagan carried 49 states and a near-record number of electoral votes.

Reagan's foreign policy showed some vulnerability as U.S.-Soviet relations failed to improve, his Lebanon policy came under fire, and his Central American policy was attacked in Congress and by the media.

The Reagan administration shifted national policy on enforcement of civil rights laws. Racial quotas for the promotion of blacks were officially renounced, and forced busing was put on a back burner.

The president was attacked relentlessly in some quarters for his advocacy of a proposed amendment to allow prayer in public schools. An unfortunate quip by the president before his weekly radio address also created a big stir. Believing the microphone to be off, Reagan joked: "My fellow Americans, I am pleased to tell you that I've signed legislation that will outlaw Russia forever. The bombing begins in five minutes." While the joke was lighthearted and off the record, it created tremors in some areas of the political world.

It's a historic realignment in fundamental party politics...

THE WALLET VOTE

Genuine Donkey and Elephant hide

'84

CORKY TRINIDAD

CORKY
Courtesy Honolulu Star–Bulletin

STEVE SACK
Courtesy Minneapolis Tribune

PAUL SZEP
Courtesy Boston Globe

'I've seen your movies and TV shows ... but I just love the way you play an American President best!'

TERRY MOSHER (AISLIN)
Courtesy Montreal Gazette

LOU GRANT
Oakland Tribune
© L. A. Times Syndicate

JEFF MACNELLY
Courtesy Chicago Tribune

ROB LAWLOR
Courtesy Philadelphia Daily News

TOM ENGELHARDT
Courtesy St. Louis Post–Dispatch

Poll Sitter

CHARLES BISSELL
Courtesy The Tennessean

"WELL, NOW, HOW ABOUT THAT?"

JOHN BRANCH
Courtesy San Antonio Express–News

BILL SANDERS
Courtesy Milwaukee Journal

BILL GRAHAM
Courtesy Arkansas Gazette

ADRIAN RAESIDE
Courtesy Times—Colonist (B.C.)

MILT PRIGGEE
Courtesy Dayton Journal–Herald

JOHN DEERING
Courtesy Arkansas Democrat

21

TAXES

Reagan to Raise Taxes Only as a 'Last Resort'

But Not on Personal Income, He Says; Will Try to Reduce Deficit With Spending Cuts Instead

EDGAR (SOL) SOLLER
Courtesy California Examiner

The Real Winner

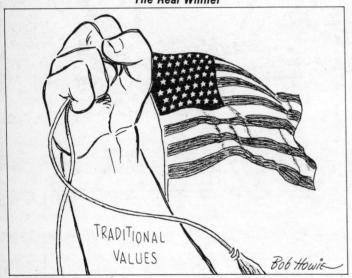

TRADITIONAL VALUES

BOB HOWIE
© Bob Howie Graphics

TOM ENGELHARDT
Courtesy St. Louis Post–Dispatch

ADMINISTRATION'S SLEAZE FACTORY

FERRARO'S FINANCES

DON'T COME IN

Wick
Casey
Meese
Allen
Thayer
Wm. F. Smith
Burford
Lavelle

'Thank Goodness All The Inspectors Are Over There And We Can Keep On With Our Work'

PHIL BISSELL
Courtesy Lowell (Mass.) Sun

TIMOTHY ATSEFF
Courtesy Syracuse Herald–Journal

HY ROSEN
Courtesy Albany Times–Union

HOW ELECTIONS ARE WON AND LOST

BILL SANDERS
Courtesy Milwaukee Journal

23

STEVE ARTLEY
Courtesy Agri News

WALT HANDELSMAN
© Patuxent Publishing Corp.

24

BOB ENGLEHART
Courtesy Hartford Courant

JIM BORGMAN
Courtesy Cincinnati Enquirer

PAUL DUGINSKI
Courtesy Sacramento Bee

SIGNE WILKINSON
Courtesy San Jose Mercury–News

BOB TAYLOR
Courtesy Dallas Times–Herald

"Gosh, Mr. President, I don't want to talk about the deficit and interest rates either, but...

ETTA HULME
Courtesy Ft. Worth Star–Telegram

THE PRESIDENT IS NOW READY TO FIELD QUESTIONS FROM THE CAMPAIGN PRESS.

JOHN BACKDERF
© Rothco

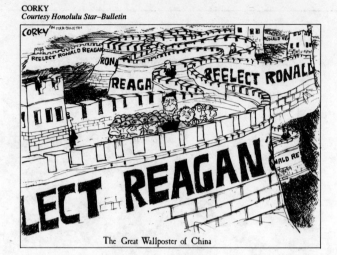

CORKY
Courtesy Honolulu Star–Bulletin

The Great Wallposter of China

GREAT MOMENTS IN AMERICAN HISTORY — By El Dani ©1984

AN ON THE SIXTH DAY OF NOVEMBER,1984 A.D. (AL-ARMED DEMOCRATS), THE PROPHETS SURVEYED THE VAST REPUBLIC AND SAW THAT IT WAS GOOD...

AND THE SAGELY,AGELESS GREAT COMMUNICATOR SAW THE SELF-SAME GOODNESS AND CAST HIS OWN VOTE, THEN RETREATED TO REST...

AND AT THE APPOINTED HOURS, GREAT WERE THE MULTITUDES THAT ALSO CAST THEIR VOTES, AND GREATER YET WAS THE TILT OF THE LAND...

AND WHEN THE TILT WAS COMPLETE,THE LAND TOOK THE FORM OF A VISAGE, VICTORIOUS,AND SPOKE: "FOUR MORE YEARS..."

© el dani Aguila
NY FILIPINO REPORTER

DANI AGUILA
Courtesy Filipino Reporter

Mondale
and the Democrats

Walter F. Mondale, the Democratic nominee for president, chose a woman—Rep. Geraldine Ferraro of New York—as his vice-presidential running mate for the first time in history. Mondale was the survivor of a long and heated Democratic campaign that went down to the wire, with Sen. Gary Hart and Jesse Jackson still in the running at the party's convention in San Francisco in July.

Hart steadfastly refused to concede the nomination until the last moment and made a last-ditch effort to woo delegates away from Mondale. Jackson entered the race in November 1983 and made headlines when he flew to Damascus, Syria, and secured the release of Lt. Robert Goodman, a U.S. Navy pilot shot down by Syrian forces in Lebanon. But Jackson sometimes suffered from the antics of supporters such as the outspoken Louis Farrakhan, and his Rainbow Coalition failed to deliver him the nomination.

Most of the attention, however, was focused on Ferraro—particularly on her finances and those of her husband. Her congressional disclosure forms affirmed that she took no part in her husband's businesses and derived no benefit from them, but her tax returns revealed that she was a part owner, vice-president, and secretary-treasurer. She dismissed the inconsistency as inconsequential. Her husband, John Zaccaro, was fined by the Federal Election Commission for having made an illegal loan of $130,000 to Ferraro's 1978 political campaign. Zaccaro's other business activities were being investigated at year's end.

STEVE BENSON
Courtesy Arizona Republic

TOM CURTIS
Courtesy Heritage Features

JIM BERRY
© NEA

"I suppose it's only right that the 'veal Mondale' was good but not exciting!"

DICK LOCHER
Courtesy Chicago Tribune

"DEFINE MY WHAT??" PAUL SZEP
Courtesy Boston Globe

ED GAMBLE
Courtesy Florida Times–Union

WAYNE STAYSKAL
Courtesy Tampa Tribune

BOB ENGLEHART
Courtesy Hartford Courant

ROB LAWLOR
Courtesy Philadelphia Daily News

BERT WHITMAN
Courtesy Phoenix Gazette

LADY IN WHITE

JIM LANGE
Courtesy Daily Oklahoman

BOB GORRELL
Courtesy Richmond News Leader

BLAINE
Courtesy The Spectator (Ont.)

STEVE KELLEY
Courtesy San Diego Union

TOM CURTIS
Courtesy Heritage Features

JIM PALMER
Courtesy Montgomery Advertiser

35

MIKE SHELTON
Courtesy Orange County
Register

CHUCK ASAY
Courtesy Colorado Springs Sun

EDDIE GERMANO
Courtesy Brockton Daily Enterprise

DOUG MACGREGOR
Courtesy Norwich Bulletin

STEVE GREENBERG
Courtesy Los Angeles Daily News

JIMMY MARGULIES
Houston Post
© Rothco

TOM CURTIS
Courtesy National Review

"*This one's for hugging Assad, this one's for hugging Castro, this one's . . .*"

JERRY BYRD
Courtesy Beaumont Enterprise

JIM BERRY
© NEA

"LOOK! THE EMPEROR HAS NO...."

THE UNCOMMITTED DEMOCRATS

PAYNE
EUGENE PAYNE
Courtesy Charlotte Observer

GARY BROOKINS
Courtesy Richmond Times–Dispatch

BROOKINS · 1984 · RICHMOND TIMES · DISPATCH

YOU WERE RIGHT, FRITZ-- REAGAN DID BRING ABOUT ARMAGEDDON!...

MONDALE-FERR CAMPAIGN HEAD

THE DAY AFTER

His roundhouse right

JON KENNEDY
Courtesy Arkansas Democrat

STEVE KELLEY
Courtesy San Diego Union

DAN WASSERMAN
© Los Angeles Times Syndicate

1984 THE RICHMOND NEWS LEADER
NEWS AMERICA SYNDICATE

BOB GORRELL
Courtesy Richmond News Leader

"@#*!! REAGAN!"

JIM LARRICK
Courtesy Columbus Dispatch

JACK JÜRDEN
*Courtesy Wilmington Evening
Journal–News*

DANA SUMMERS
Courtesy Orlando Sentinel

'GERALDINE!!'

JON KENNEDY
Courtesy Arkansas Democrat

DICK LOCHER
Courtesy Chicago Tribune

RICHARD CROWSON
Courtesy Jackson (Tenn.) Sun

AL LIEDERMAN
© Rothco

45

JEFF MACNELLY
Courtesy Chicago Tribune

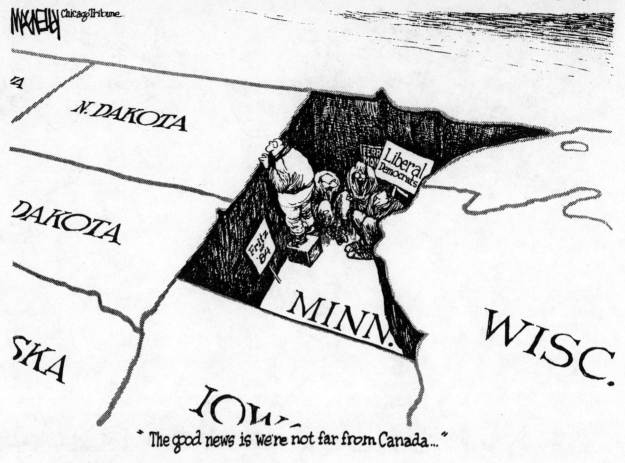

"The good news is we're not far from Canada..."

TOM FLANNERY
Courtesy Baltimore Sun

"WE WANT TO STAY AND SEE IT AGAIN"

The Presidential Debates

Two so-called debates were televised nationwide during the 1984 campaign between the presidential contenders, and one was staged between the candidates for vice-president.

On October 7, Walter Mondale and Ronald Reagan squared off in Louisville, Kentucky, and fielded questions concerning domestic issues. There was general agreement that Mondale emerged the narrow winner, and the perceived victory appeared to give his faltering campaign a boost—at least temporarily.

Four days later, Vice-President George Bush shared a similar platform with the Democratic vice-presidential nominee, Geraldine Ferraro, in Philadelphia. Most polls afterward gave the edge to Bush.

Reagan and Mondale met a second time on October 21 in Kansas City to debate foreign affairs. The president had looked old and tired in the first encounter but came back strongly in Kansas City, looking vigorous and "in charge." The fact that Reagan did not fall on his face virtually ended Mondale's hopes for the presidency.

The debates proved much more popular with viewers than the party conventions held earlier in the year. Each debate attracted an estimated audience of more than eighty million people.

BOB ENGLEHART
Courtesy Hartford Courant

DRAPER HILL
Courtesy Detroit News

JOHN STAMPONE
Courtesy Clearwater Sun

JACK JURDEN
*Courtesy Wilmington Evening
Journal–News*

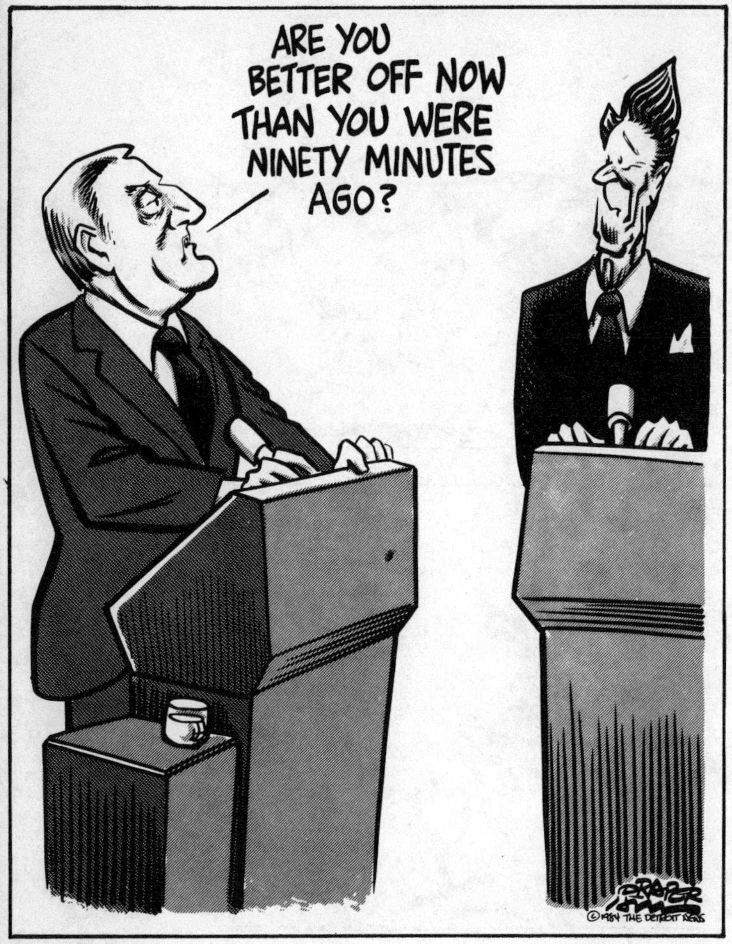
ARE YOU BETTER OFF NOW THAN YOU WERE NINETY MINUTES AGO?
DRAPER
© 1984 THE DETROIT NEWS

DRAPER HILL
Courtesy Detroit News

RALPH DUNAGIN
Courtesy Orlando Sentinel

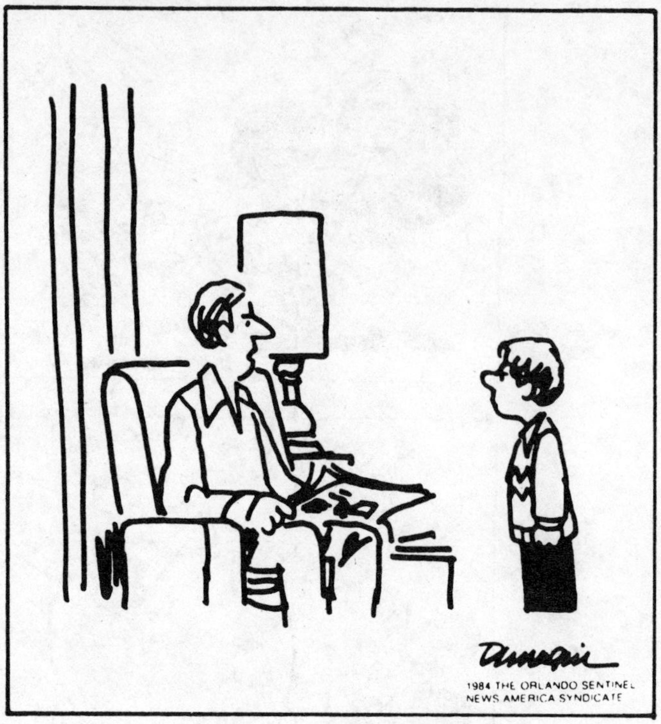
DUNAGIN
1984 THE ORLANDO SENTINEL
NEWS AMERICA SYNDICATE

"YOU DON'T GET A REBUTTAL."

JIM LARRICK
Courtesy Columbus Dispatch

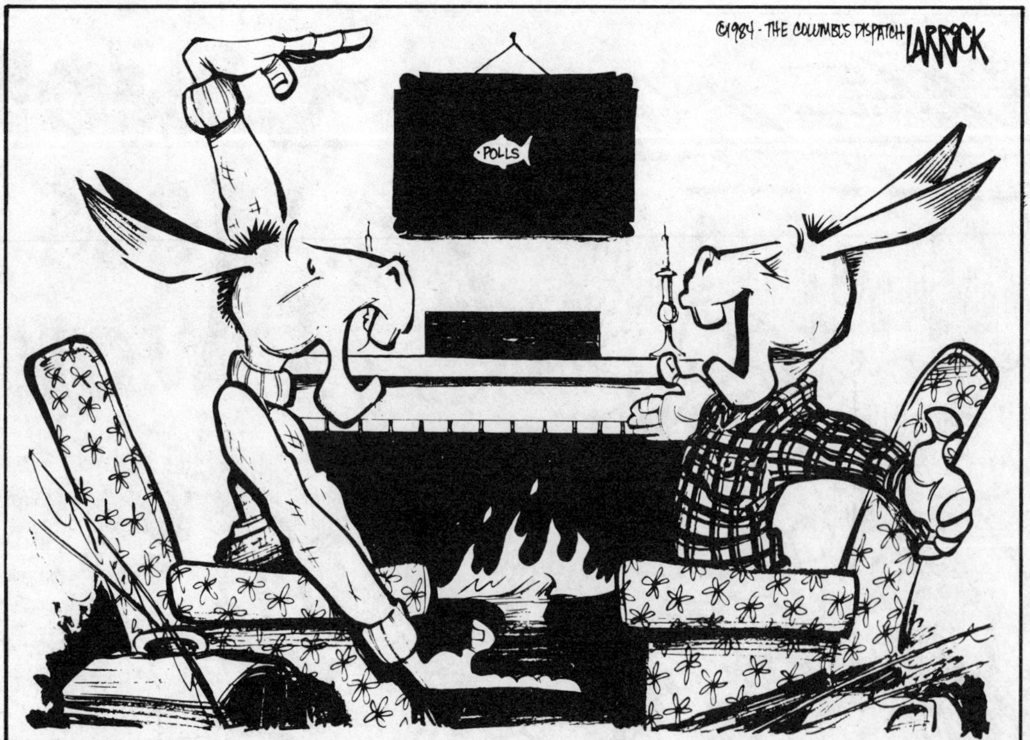
©1984 - THE COLUMBUS DISPATCH
LARRICK
POLLS

DEBATE STORIES

U.S. Congress

The 1984 elections produced a virtual standoff in Congress, with the Democrats picking up two seats in the Senate and the Republicans failing to gain enough seats in the House to make a real difference.

In the most expensive U.S. Senate contest in history, ultra-conservative incumbent Jesse Helms withstood a stiff challenge by liberal Democrat Gov. James B. Hunt, Jr. The two candidates spent a total of almost $23 million.

Congress devoted considerable attention during the year to the touchy issue of school prayer. Nothing was settled, however, as proponents failed to push through two proposals that would have added a constitutional amendment allowing organized prayer in schools.

A civil rights bill attempting to reverse a Supreme Court ruling on discrimination in education passed the House but failed in the Senate. The court had ruled that antidiscrimination laws affecting some programs at an institution did not apply to the institution as a whole. The Congress also failed to reach agreement on how to deal with the problem of massive illegal immigration.

New laws alleviated the problems of farmers whose assets could have been tied up indefinitely in bankruptcy cases, and new legislation widened eligibility requirements for disability benefits. The Reagan administration cut more than 500,000 from welfare rolls, but more than half were restored by congressional action.

"WAIT A MINUTE UNTIL I EXTEND THIS BRIDGE A LITTLE FARTHER!"

CHUCK BROOKS
Courtesy Birmingham News

STEVE KELLEY
Courtesy San Diego Union

JERRY BARNETT
Courtesy Indianapolis News

RALPH DUNAGIN
Courtesy Orlando Sentinel

"WE JUST SPENT $12 MILLION TO CONVINCE THE POOR PEOPLE YOU'RE NOT RICH!"

ART WOOD
Courtesy AFBF (D.C.)

DICK WRIGHT
© Scripps-Howard Newspapers

LEE JUDGE
Courtesy Kansas City Times

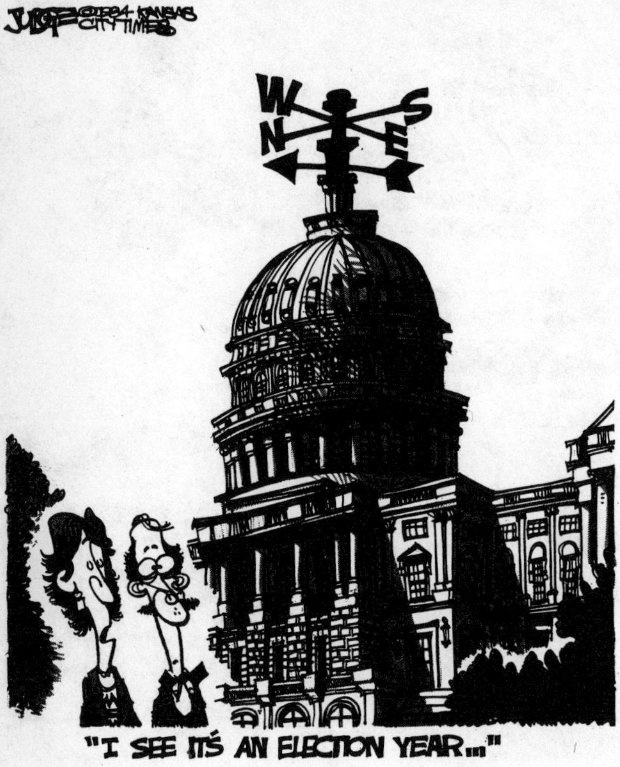
W
S
N
E
"I SEE IT'S AN ELECTION YEAR..."

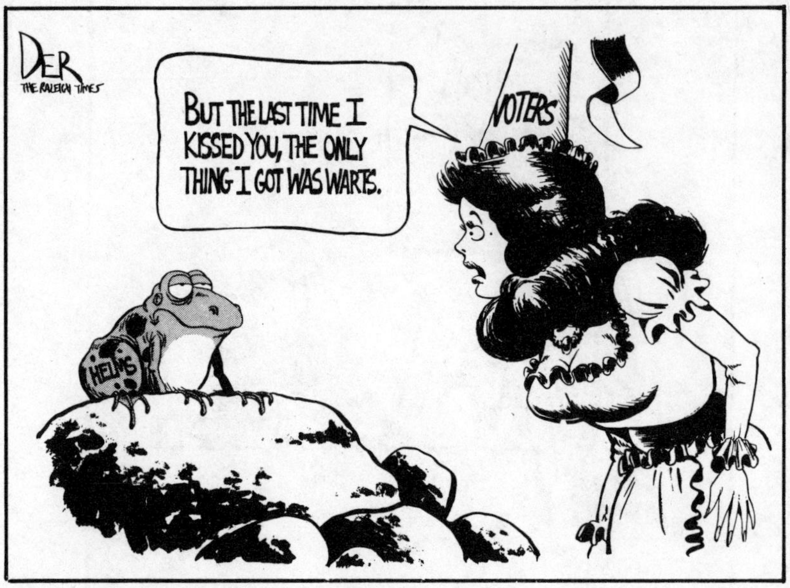
DER THE RALEIGH TIMES
BUT THE LAST TIME I KISSED YOU, THE ONLY THING I GOT WAS WARTS.
VOTERS
HELMS

LAMBERT DER
Courtesy Raleigh Times

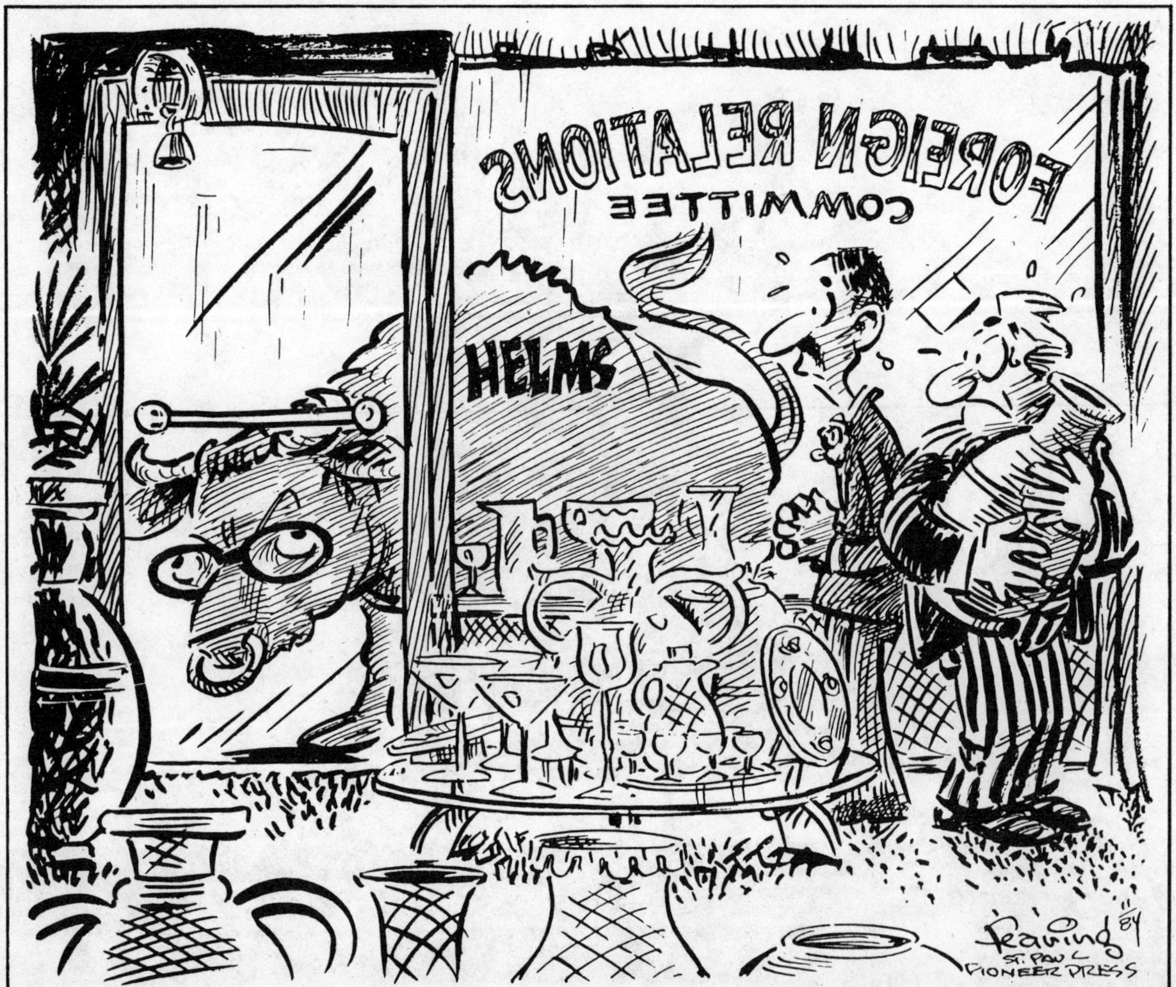
FOREIGN RELATIONS COMMITTEE
HELMS
Fearing '84 ST. PAUL PIONEER PRESS

JERRY FEARING
Courtesy St. Paul Dispatch–Pioneer Press

U.S. Defense

Arms control talks between the United States and the Soviet Union remained in cold storage during 1984, but President Reagan's reelection in November prompted an announcement that preliminary talks on resuming negotiations would be held early in 1985. The Soviets had walked out of arms control talks in late 1983 when NATO began the deployment of U.S. cruise and Pershing II nuclear missiles in Western Europe.

During the year the U.S. sped up the development of weapons that would be used to fight a space war. In June, a dummy missile warhead was intercepted and destroyed by a new type of antiballistic missile in a test over the Pacific Ocean. The Pentagon seemed ready to move ahead aggressively with Reagan's "Star Wars" concept. The Pentagon reported in June that the U.S.S.R. had surpassed the U.S. in the number of nuclear warheads.

Highly publicized stories about overpricing and the poor quality of weapons continued, many of them prompted by official leaks. The military was found to be paying $7,622 apiece for ten-cup coffee makers and $171 for small flashlights.

President Reagan requested $313.4 billion for defense spending in 1985; Congress trimmed the amount to $297 billion.

MIKE PETERS
Courtesy Dayton Daily News

LARRY WRIGHT
Courtesy Detroit News

DARCY
Newsday cartoon by Tom Darcy

'Daddy, does the arms race have a finish line?'

TOM DARCY
Courtesy Newsday

DANA SUMMERS
Courtesy Orlando Sentinel

RAY OSRIN
Courtesy Cleveland Plain Dealer

CREATIVE FINANCING   **HEADACHE REMEDY**   **PEACEKEEPER**

The Budget Deficit

The federal deficit for fiscal 1984, which ended on September 30, rose to an unprecedented $175.3 billion. The Congressional Budget Office estimated that the deficit would grow to $263 billion by fiscal 1989 unless Congress cut spending drastically or raised taxes. The CBO, along with economists and businessmen across the nation, maintained that such huge deficits would cause interest rates to remain too high to allow economic growth.

Chairman Paul A. Volcker of the Federal Reserve Board announced on July 25 a decision not to tighten the nation's money supply. The Fed began to infuse funds into the economy in late September, and large banks immediately began to lower their rates.

President Reagan proposed a 1985 budget of $925.5 billion, with revenues of $745.1 billion. At the same time he proposed a deficit reduction of $100 billion, to come from tax increases and spending cuts over three years. Congress voted to boost taxes by about $50 billion over the same period and called for $13 billion in spending reductions. As the year ended, the projected deficit for 1985 was revised upward to $215 billion. The issue would clearly be the number-one priority for the new Congress.

ED ASHLEY
Courtesy Toledo Blade

REAGAN'S PLAN FOR DEALING WITH THE DEFICIT

ETTA HULME
Courtesy Ft. Worth Star–Telegram

J. D. CROWE
Courtesy Ft. Worth Star–Telegram

TAXES DON'T HAVE TO BE RAISED— WE CAN MOVE DOWN A FEW FLOORS!

CHUCK BROOKS
Courtesy Birmingham News

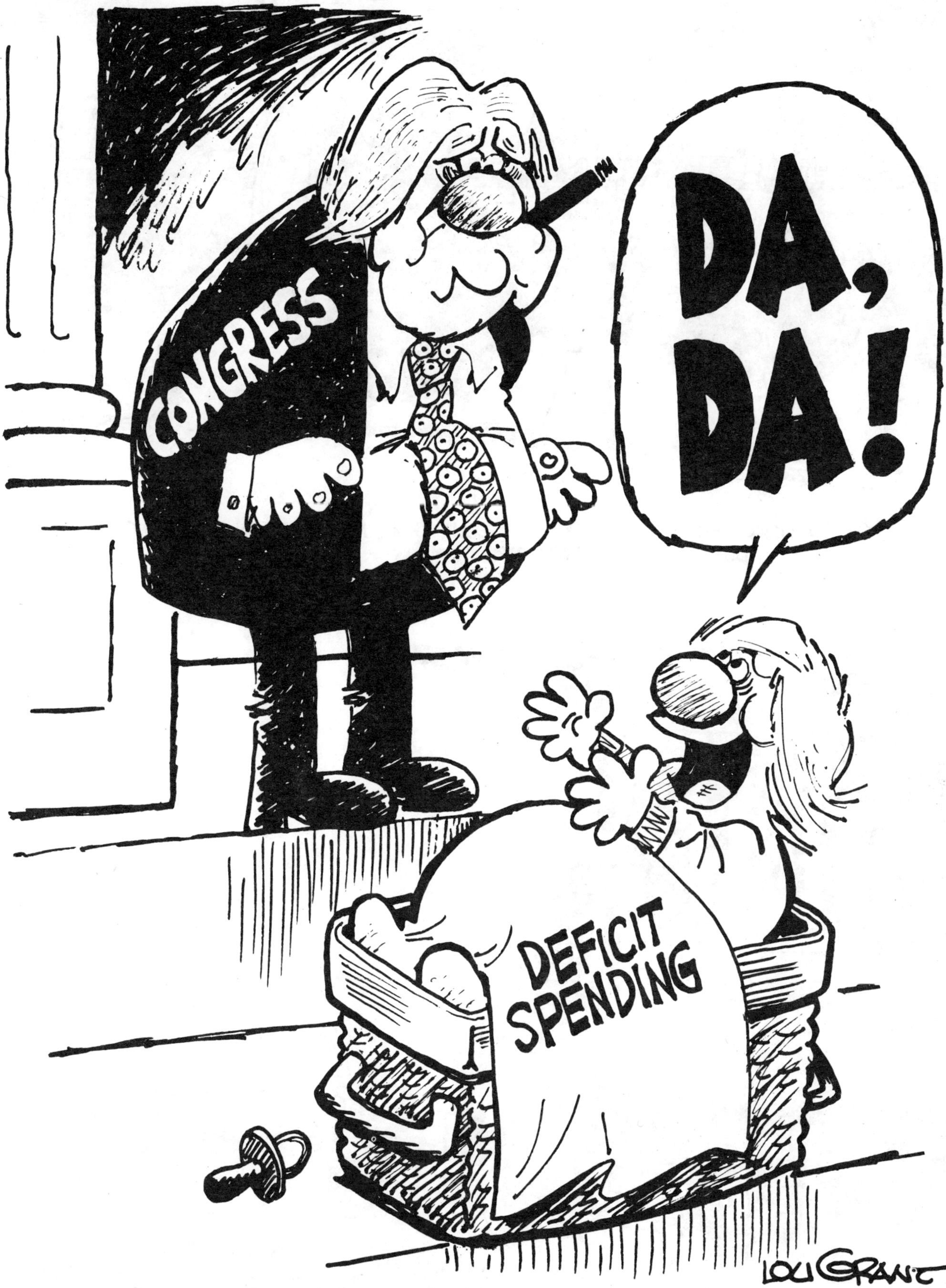
CONGRESS
DA, DA!
DEFICIT SPENDING
LOU GRANT

LOU GRANT
Oakland Tribune

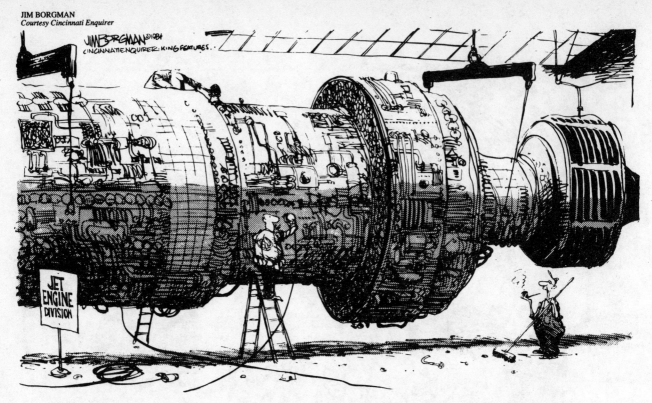

" YEP, I PICK UP ALL THESE LITTLE DOOHICKIES YOU FELLAS DROP... MADE FOURTEEN MILLION BUCKS LAST YEAR IN THE SPARE PARTS BUSINESS. "

"HANG IN THERE—I'M WORKING ON A CURE"

MIDDLE INCOME TAXPAYER

TAX REFORM

LOU GRANT
Oakland Tribune
© L. A. Times Syndicate

"THE BALANCED BUDGET"

LAMBERT DER
Courtesy Raleigh Times

STATE OF THE UNION

DEFICIT

JERRY FEARING
Courtesy St. Paul Dispatch–
Pioneer Press

The Economy

The solid economic recovery that began in 1983 picked up steam and turned into a boom during the first half of 1984. Inflation remained under control at 3.7 percent, while business activity and consumer buying surged upward. But as the action rolled along on a high economic note, financial analysis expressed concern about the huge federal deficit and the wisdom of administration politics intended to push the recovery along.

The U.S. dollar remained super-strong. As its strength made imports cheaper, U.S. exports became more expensive overseas, creating a record-setting projected trade deficit of $130 billion for 1984. The flow of $80 billion in foreign capital into the U.S., largely because of high interest rates, offset the trade deficit somewhat. The Gross National Product soared to a 10.1 percent annual rate in the first quarter, rumbled along to a 7.1 percent mark in the second quarter, dipped to only 1.9 percent in the third quarter, but finished strongly in the final period.

Harvested crops for the year were above average, but livestock producers were forced to cut inventories because of rising grain prices. Small livestock farmers, of course, were caught in the squeeze.

In June, Walt Disney Productions, one of the country's largest corporations, managed to fend off an attempted takeover by a group headed by New York financier Saul P. Steinberg, but it was expensive. The would-be purchasers wound up with a profit of $31.7 million.

JIM BORGMAN
Courtesy Cincinnati Enquirer

"WE INTERRUPT THIS PROGRAM FOR ANOTHER BULLETIN ON THE ECONOMIC RECOVERY..."

Administration Pleased at Economy Slow Down Rate.

JIM DOBBINS
Courtesy Union–Leader

TOM ENGELHARDT
Courtesy St. Louis Post–Dispatch

Offshore Exploration

JACK MCLEOD
© Army Times

65

"NOW DO YOU BELIEVE I'VE GOT HIM UNDER CONTROL?"

GENE BASSET
Courtesy Atlanta Journal

KEN ALEXANDER
San Francisco Examiner
© Copley News Service

BILL GARNER
Courtesy Washington Times

ART WOOD
Courtesy AFBF (D.C.)

ROB LAWLOR
Courtesy Philadelphia Daily News

67

JEFF KOTERBA
Courtesy Kearney
Daily Hub (Neb.)

BRIAN GABLE
Courtesy Regina Leader–Post (Sask.)

ED FI3CHER
Courtesy Rochester Post–Bulletin

JOSEPH HELLER
Courtesy West Bend News (Wisc.)

MUTT AND JEFF

ART WOOD
Courtesy AFBF (D.C.)

BERT WHITMAN
Courtesy Phoenix Gazette

SAD COMMENTARY ON THE VIRTUES OF HANKY PANKY

JON KENNEDY
Courtesy Arkansas Democrat

'On *second* thought—'

U.S. Foreign Policy

Relations between the United States and the Soviet Union remained at low ebb during most of 1984, primarily because of the deployment of Pershing II and cruise missiles by the U.S. in Western Europe. The Russians had walked out of arms control talks and announced they would not return to the conference table until the missiles were withdrawn.

The U.S. declined to withdraw the weapons, and for several months various accusations were tossed about by both sides regarding who was responsible for the deterioration of relations. By midyear, however, the posture of the U.S.S.R. began to change. The Soviets requested talks with the U.S. on antisatellite weapons, and Foreign Minister Andrei Gromyko accepted an invitation to meet with President Reagan at the White House. About this time, Reagan altered his approach. Careful to mask any hostility, he and other administration officials repeatedly underscored the need for dialogue between the two powers. Eventually it was announced that Gromyko would meet with U.S. Secretary of State George Shultz in Geneva in 1985 to work out an agenda for future arms talks.

The International Court of Justice ruled in favor of a restraining order against U.S. military activities aimed at Nicaragua, including the mining of Nicaraguan ports. However, the U.S. denied that the World Court had jurisdiction in the matter.

BOB TAYLOR
Courtesy Dallas Times–Herald

ELDON PLETCHER
Courtesy New Orleans Times–Picayune

JIM BORGMAN
Courtesy Cincinnati Enquirer

"KREMLIN, SHULTZ.... I SAID I'D MEET WITH THE KREMLIN!"

V. CULLUM ROGERS
Courtesy Durham Morning Herald

CLIFF LEVERETTE
© Bob Howie Graphics

"SCENE CHANGE M.R. REAGAN. INSTEAD OF THE STRAIGHT SHOOTING COWBOY, YOU ARE HIS PEACEFUL TWIN, FATHER O'REAGAN!!"

73

GEORGE FISHER
Courtesy Arkansas Gazette

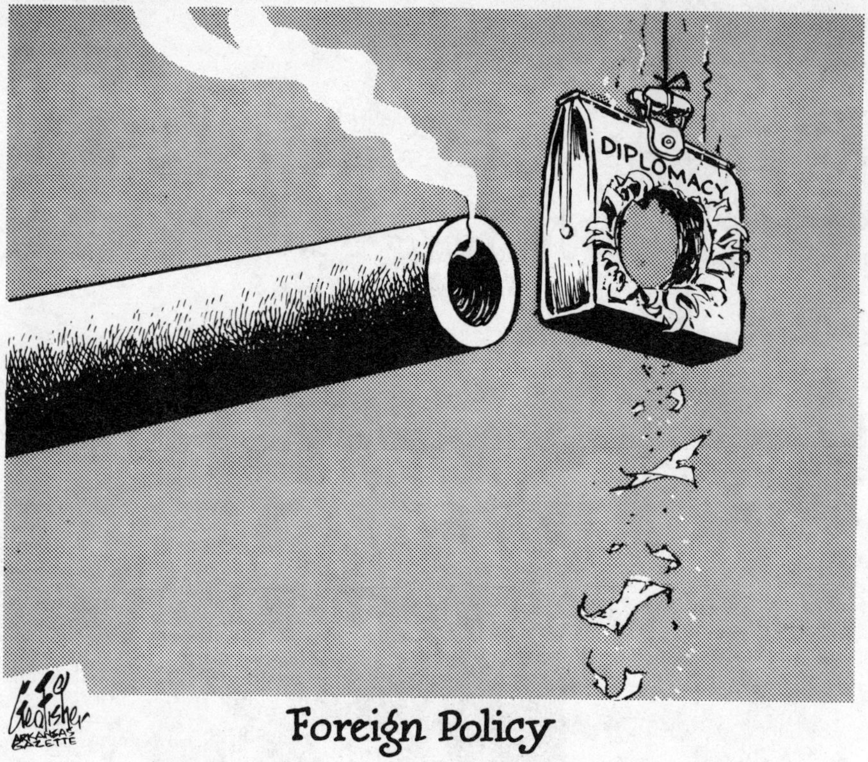
DIPLOMACY
Foreign Policy

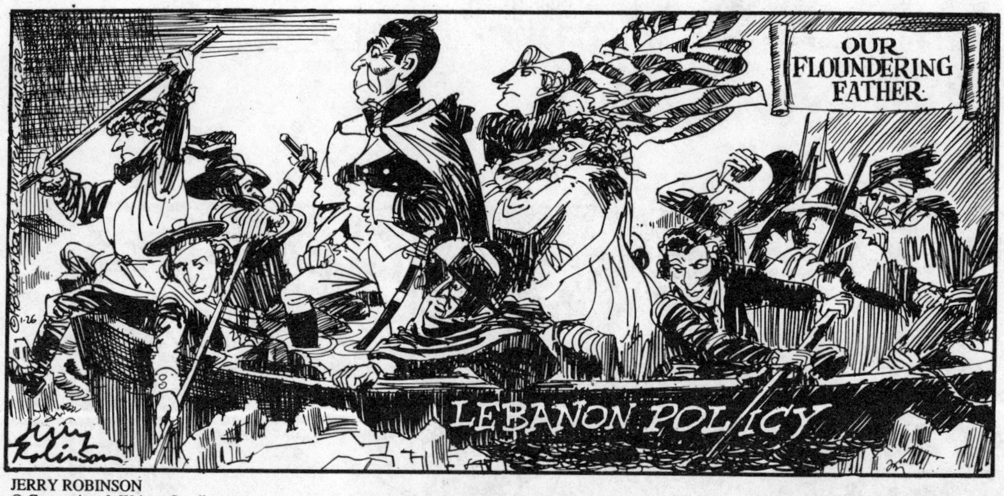
OUR FLOUNDERING FATHER
LEBANON POLICY

JERRY ROBINSON
© Cartoonists & Writers Syndicate

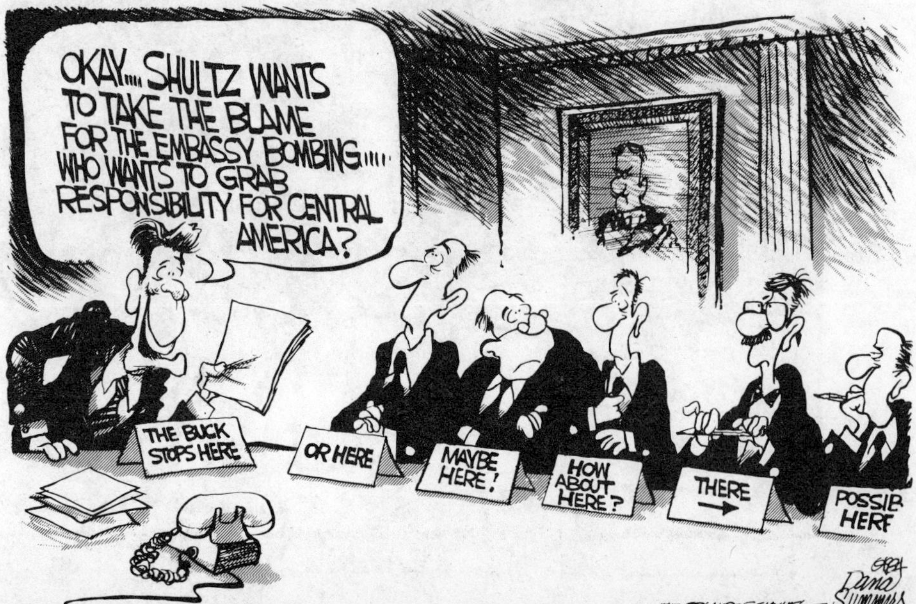
OKAY... SHULTZ WANTS TO TAKE THE BLAME FOR THE EMBASSY BOMBING..... WHO WANTS TO GRAB RESPONSIBILITY FOR CENTRAL AMERICA?
THE BUCK STOPS HERE
OR HERE
MAYBE HERE!
HOW ABOUT HERE?
THERE
POSSIB HERE

DANA SUMMERS
Courtesy Orlando Sentinel

The Third World

A probe into the 1983 assassination of the Philippines' moderate opposition leader Benigno Aquino continued well into 1984, and in late October investigators' findings were released. Pres. Ferdinand E. Marcos had gained a modicum of credibility by permitting a relatively free investigation of the incident. The investigators concluded that Aquino had been killed as the result of a military plot. Several top members of the military were implicated, including Gen. Fabian C. Ver, armed forces chief of staff and a close friend of Marcos.

Indira Gandhi, prime minister of India, was assassinated by her Sikh bodyguards on October 31 at her home, and a bloodbath was unleashed against Sikhs across India. Mrs. Gandhi's son Rajiv, 40, was named the new prime minister.

The combination of a terrible drought and the callousness and ineptness of the ruling Marxist government sent a devastating famine across Ethiopia, with perhaps hundreds of thousands starving to death and millions more in peril. The Marxist leaders had spent some $200 million on an anniversary celebration, but claimed poverty and an inability to feed the people. The world, particularly the United States, responded generously, but in many cases food shipments were delayed or confiscated after reaching Ethiopia. It was alleged that Ethiopia was selling some of the food to neighboring countries.

DANI AGUILA
Courtesy Filipino Reporter

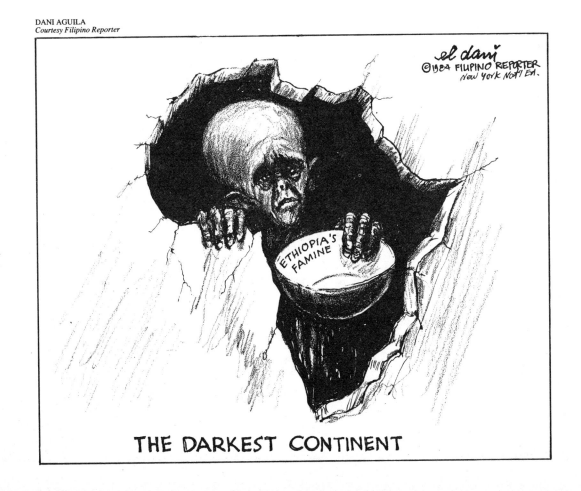

THE DARKEST CONTINENT

JIM KNUDSEN
Courtesy L.A. Tidings

AID

BILL SANDERS
Courtesy Milwaukee Journal

Madonna and Child

KAL
The Observer (London, Eng.)
© Cartoonists and Writers Syndicate

JOSH BEUTEL
Courtesy Saint John
Telegraph–Journal

...MORE WIDESPREAD DEATH AND FAMINE BRINGS THE ETHIOPIAN DEATH COUNT TO 200,000... NOW A WORD FROM OUR SPONSOR...

...BURGERMACMONSTER! THAT JUICY, MOUTHWATERING TRIPLE DECKER... OVER THIRTY BILLION SOLD

ROB LAWLOR
Courtesy Philadelphia Daily News

H. CLAY BENNETT
Courtesy St. Petersburg Times

MIKE KEEFE
Courtesy Denver Post

JOSH BEUTEL
*Courtesy Saint John
  Telegraph–Journal*

HY ROSEN
Courtesy Albany Times–Union

CHUCK AYERS
Courtesy Akron Beacon–Journal

MIKE GRASTON
Courtesy Windsor Star (Ont.)

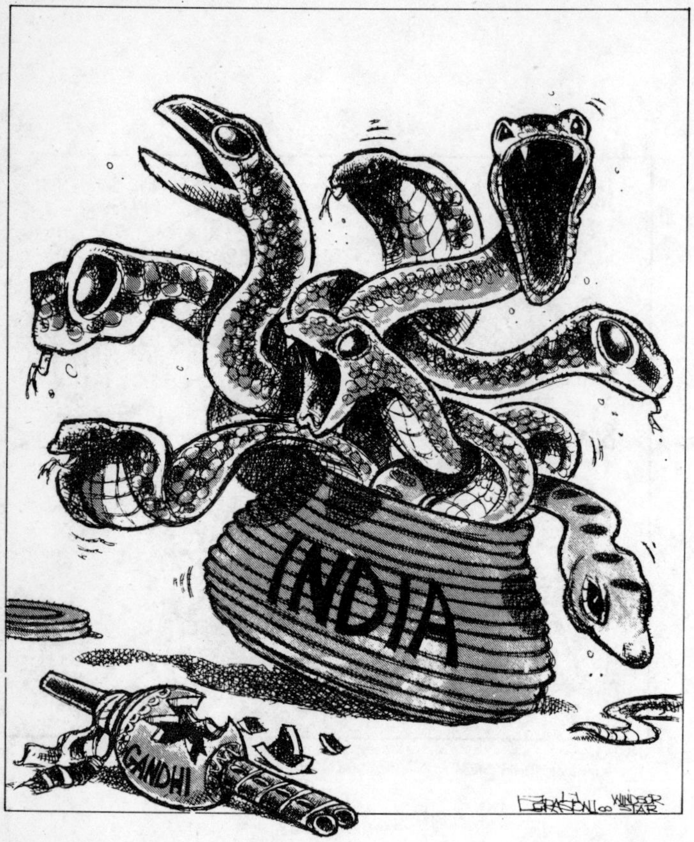
INDIA
GANDHI
WINDSOR STAR

CORKY
Courtesy Honolulu Star–Bulletin

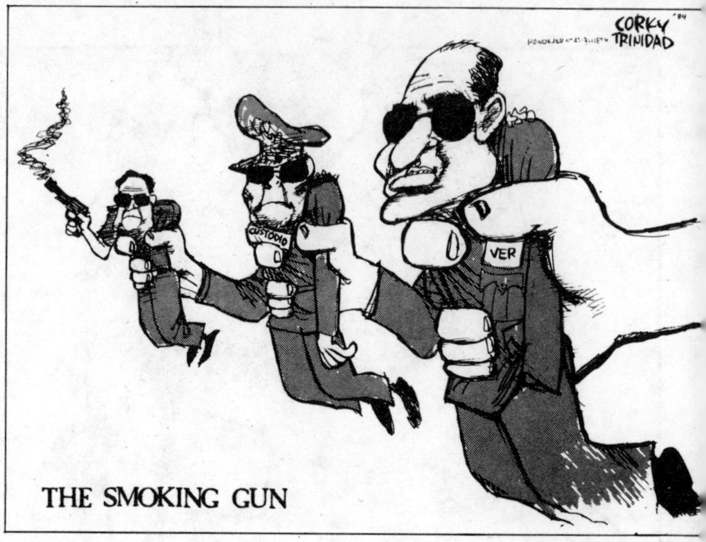
CORKY '84 TRINIDAD
CUSTODIO
VER
THE SMOKING GUN

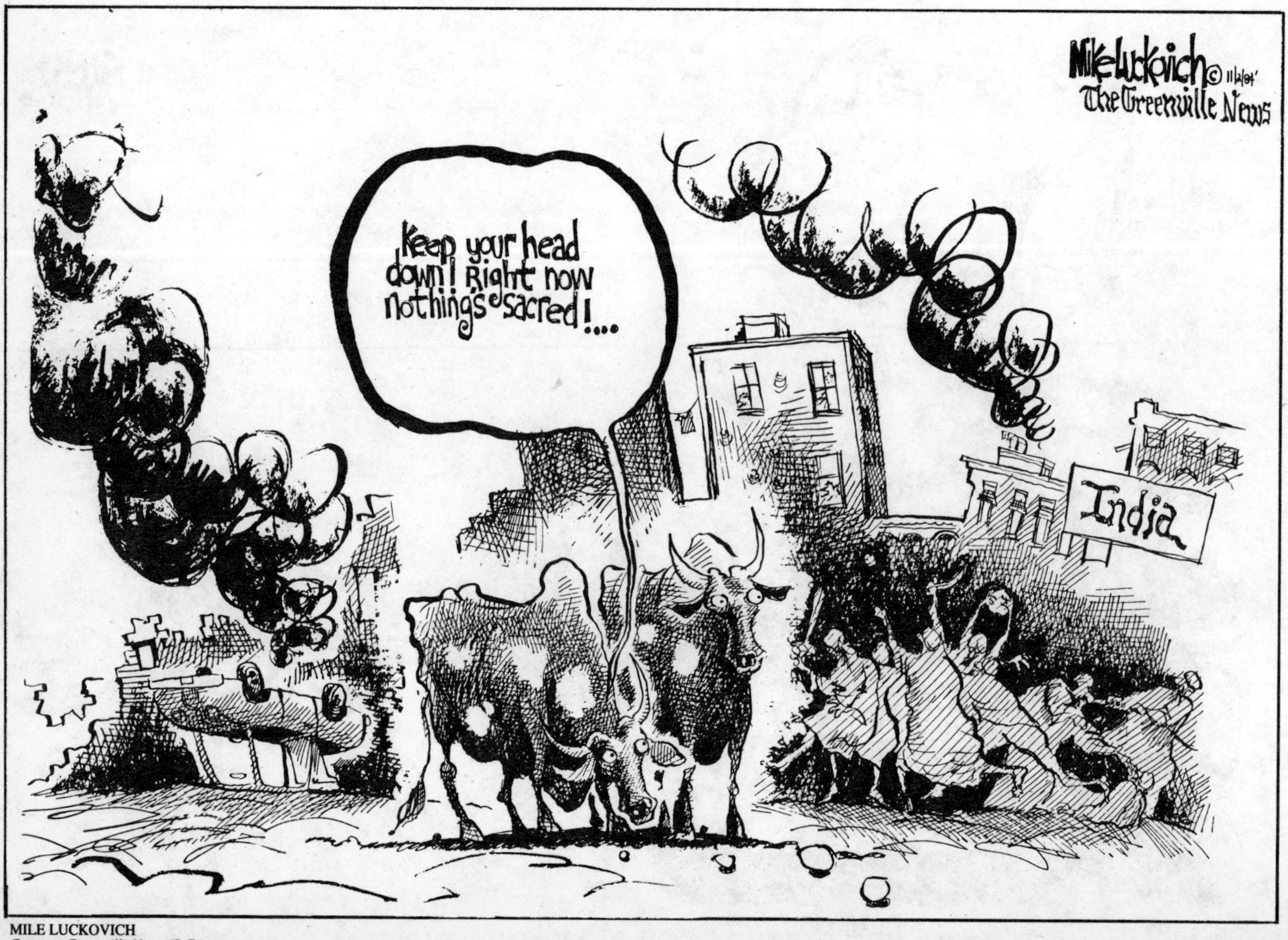
Mike Luckovich © 11/2/84
The Greenville News
Keep your head down! Right now nothing's sacred!....
India

MILE LUCKOVICH
Courtesy Greenville News (S.C.)

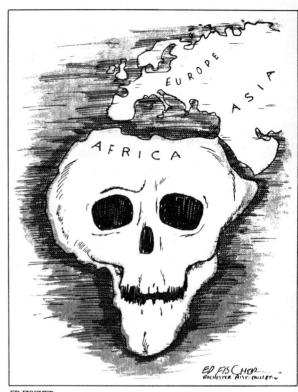

DICK WALLMEYER
Courtesy Independent Press–Telegram
(Calif.)

ED FISCHER
Courtesy Rochester Post–Bulletin

STEVE SACK
Courtesy Minneapolis Tribune

81

The Mideast

After the rebellion within the ranks staged against Palestine Liberation Organization Chairman Yasir Arafat in 1983, many observers assumed that the controversial figure was finished as a leader of the PLO. In early 1984, however, he launched a major campaign to reunify Palestinian ranks and regain his authority.

Several major incidents occurred in the Mideast during the year, including Palestinian acts of violence and terrorism committed in Israel and the Israeli-occupied West Bank and Gaza Strip, but it was never established that the PLO was responsible for the ruthless acts. On the whole, the PLO's ability to mount serious threats against Israel seemed to have diminished.

The new Israeli government was based on a unique arrangement. The Labor Party's Shimon Peres became prime minister, and Likud Party leader Yitzhak Shamir was named foreign minister. At the half-way mark of the administration, the two were slated to switch jobs.

Iraq and Iran entered the fifth year of their costly war, with neither side seeming capable of defeating the other. Diplomatic relations between Libya and Great Britain were severed after several shootings and bombings in Britain in which Libyans were believed to have been involved.

CHUCK AYERS
Courtesy Akron Beacon-Journal

PAUL SZEP
Courtesy Boston Globe

JEFF MACNELLY
Courtesy Chicago Tribune

IRANIANS CLAIM CAPABILITY TO MAKE THEIR OWN CHEMICAL ARMS

STEVE LINDSTROM
Courtesy Duluth News–Tribune

"TO BE HONEST, I DIDN'T EVEN KNOW LEBANON _HAD_ A HOCKEY TEAM."

TIMOTHY ATSEFF
Courtesy Syracuse Herald–Journal

JOHN R. THORNTON
Courtesy Republican Journal

JERRY ROBINSON
© Cartoonists & Writers Syndicate

MILT PRIGGEE
Courtesy Dayton Journal–Herald

JIM LARRICK
Courtesy Columbus Dispatch

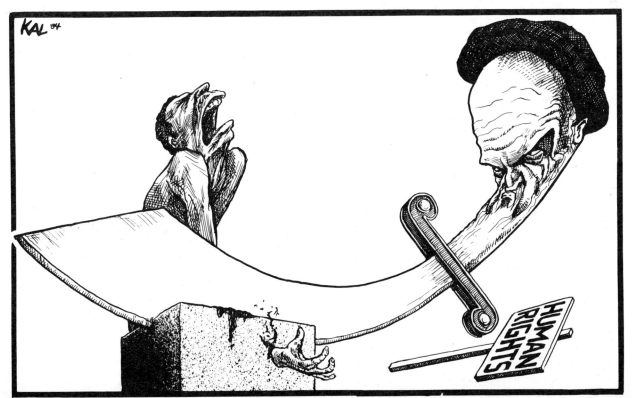

KAL
The Observer (London, Eng.)
© Cartoonists and Writers Syndicate

Sacramento Bee

'I've got an ugly scar like that; it spells 'Vietnam.''

ISRAEL DECIDES TO WITHDRAW FROM LEBANON, UNILATERALLY.

Central America

Congress offered a more receptive ear to administration requests for aid to El Salvador during the year, but it was less willing to support U.S. intervention in Nicaragua. After moderate Jose Napoleon Duarte defeated his right-wing opponent in El Salvador's May election, Congress voted to authorize even more funds for military aid to that nation than President Reagan had requested.

When word got out in April that the Central Intelligence Agency had directed the mining of several Nicaraguan ports, Congress expressed outrage and passed non-binding resolutions condemning the action. The Senate joined the House in continuing through February 1985 a ban on aid to the Contras in their attempts to overthrow the leftist Sandinistas.

Mexico slowly began emerging from a deep and long-standing economic depression and announced a new drive to eradicate corruption in government and business and to bring about massive educational reforms. President Miguel de la Madrid Hurtado initiated a strict program of austerity that reduced inflation from 80 percent to 50 percent and pared Mexico's $96 billion debt to foreign banks by $13 billion. Reagan and de la Madrid met in Washington to discuss the growing problem of Mexican aliens entering the U.S. illegally.

MIKE KEEFE
Courtesy Denver Post

BEN SARGENT
Courtesy Austin American–Statesman

TOM DARCY
Courtesy Newsday

BILL GARNER
Courtesy Washington Times

MIKE PETERS
Courtesy Dayton Daily News

DANA SUMMERS
Courtesy Orlando Sentinel

TOMB OF THE UNKNOWN
SOLDIER

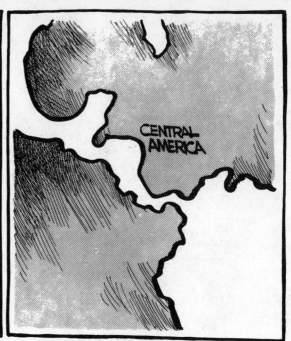

TOMB OF THE UNKNOWN
POLICY

EUGENE PAYNE
Courtesy Charlotte Observer

KIRK WALTERS
Courtesy Scranton Times

DRAPER HILL
Courtesy Detroit News

MIKE GRASTON
Courtesy Windsor Star (Ont.)

LAZARO FRESQUET
Courtesy El Miami Herald

JOHN BRANCH
Courtesy San Antonio Express–News

BOB TAYLOR
Courtesy Dallas Times–Herald

92

YOUR TAX DOLLARS AT WORK IN EL SALVADOR.

H. CLAY BENNETT
Courtesy St. Petersburg Times

KAL
The Observer (London, Eng.)
© Cartoonists and Writers Syndicate

Canadian Politics

In 1984 Canadian politics underwent the greatest change to occur in a generation. Pierre Elliott Trudeau, leader of the Liberal Party since 1968 and prime minister for virtually the entire period, announced his retirement in the summer. The election which followed saw the Progressive Conservative Party sweep into office with the largest majority in history in the House of Commons. Prime Minister Brian Mulroney was sworn into office on September 17.

Former Finance Minister John Turner and Energy Minister Jean Cretein, a powerful ally of Trudeau, led the battle for the Liberal cause, but it was apparent the voters wanted a change from the Trudeau policies. Mulroney promised to restore "a true partnership" between Canada and the U.S. and offered a firm commitment to reevaluate defense needs and trim the budget deficit.

The Canadian dollar dropped six U.S. cents, and unemployment held firm at 11 percent. High interest rates continued throughout the year, peaking at 13.26 percent in July, but the economic boom in the U.S. helped prop up Canada's trade surplus.

Pope John Paul II was warmly received on a September visit, and Queen Elizabeth II and Prince Philip made a 14-day tour late in the year.

Acid rain spawned by American and Canadian industry continued as a major problem.

BRIAN GABLE
Courtesy Regina Leader–Post (Sask.)

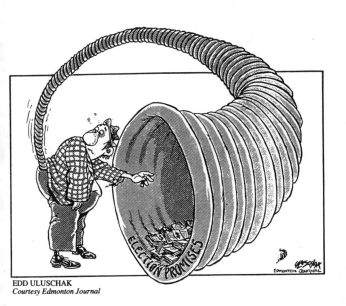

EDD ULUSCHAK
Courtesy Edmonton Journal

RAOUL HUNTER
Courtesy Le Soleil (Que.)

ROY PETERSON
Courtesy Vancouver Sun

"Okay, okay — have it your way . . . when I've achieved World Peace I'll return to drawing Doonesbury . . ."

95

"IT'S [HONEY] DIFFERENT FROM MR. TRUDEAU'S GHERKINS IN VINEGAR!"

RAOUL HUNTER
Courtesy Le Soleil (Que.)

BLAINE
Courtesy The Spectator (Ont.)

PASSING THE BUCK

WHERE'S THE TROUGH?

TERRY MOSHER (AISLIN)
Courtesy Montreal Gazette

JOSH BEUTEL
*Courtesy Saint John
Telegraph–Journal*

"There are many Canadian jobs dependent upon U.S. policy." – BRIAN MULRONEY

ADRIAN RAESIDE
Courtesy Times–Colonist (B.C.)

MERLE TINGLEY
Courtesy London Free Press (Can.)

RAOUL HUNTER
Courtesy Le Soleil (Que.)

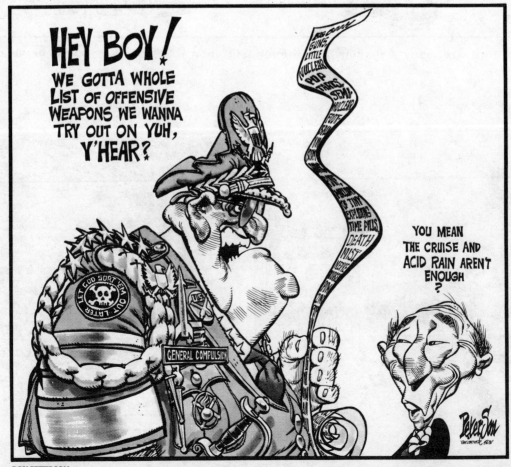

ROY PETERSON
Courtesy Vancouver Sun

The Soviet Union

The Soviet Union continued to have problems with its top leadership in 1984. As more than one American official phrased it, "They just keep dying." In February, after only 15 months in office, Communist Party General Secretary Yuri Andropov passed away. His successor, Konstantin Chernenko, 72, appeared to be in such poor health that another leadership change seemed likely at any time. Chernenko appeared feeble on television and for two months virtually dropped out of sight.

Soviet policy underwent a major change during the year as restrictions were tightened on Western contacts with dissidents and individuals attempting to emigrate. Andrei Sakharov, the Russian nuclear physicist who won the 1975 Nobel Prize, and his wife were denied visas to leave the country. He apparently was exiled to Gorky and was reported by Moscow Radio to be "alive and well," although reports that he was near death continued to surface.

In March, a planned visit by the president of the German Democratic Republic to West Germany was postponed because of pressure from the Soviets. The two Germanys had been moving toward greater cooperation in economic matters, and the hardliners in the Kremlin seemed to fear that the two countries might become too friendly.

The war in Afghanistan moved into its fifth year as civilian casualties and economic devastation continued to heighten. But the world seemed to have lost interest.

DICK LOCHER
Courtesy Chicago Tribune

MIKE PETERS
Courtesy Dayton Daily News

COMRADES, WE'VE DECIDED TO SHORTEN THE SELECTION PROCESS FOR CHAIRMAN ANDROPOV'S SUCCESSOR...

GARY BROOKINS
Courtesy Richmond Times–Dispatch

SOVIET POLITICAL LIFE

MILT PRIGGEE
Courtesy Dayton Journal–Herald

'You're the youngest---YOU take it.'

JON KENNEDY
Courtesy Arkansas Democrat

BRIAN GABLE
Courtesy Regina Leader–Post (Sask.)

BRUCE BEATTIE
*Courtesy Daytona Beach
News-Journal*

"Verification is very difficult during an election year... See if our inspection team can find out if Reagan is serious or not on arms control."

DICK WALLMEYER
*Courtesy Independent Press-Telegram
(Calif.)*

QUIET DIPLOMACY

LOOK AT ME, A WOMAN WALKING IN SPACE!

SO AM I... WHEE!

GERALDINE

AL LIEDERMAN
© Rothco

ADRIAN RAESIDE
Courtesy Times–Colonist (B.C.)

RAY OSRIN
Courtesy Cleveland Plain Dealer

"Remember, Comrade, people who are willing to destroy an efficient telephone system may not be playing with a full deck."

103

MILE LUCKOVICH
Courtesy Greenville News (S.C.)

JIM DOBBINS
Courtesy Union–Leader

G MACINTOSH
tesy Minneapolis Star–Tribune

TOM FLANNERY
Courtesy Baltimore Sun

"HERE HE'S SCOWLING,
BUT THIS COULD BE THE FEINT"

GENE BASSET
Courtesy Atlanta Journal

"DAMMIT, SAKHAROV... YOU'RE GIVING THE SOVIET UNION A BAD NAME!"

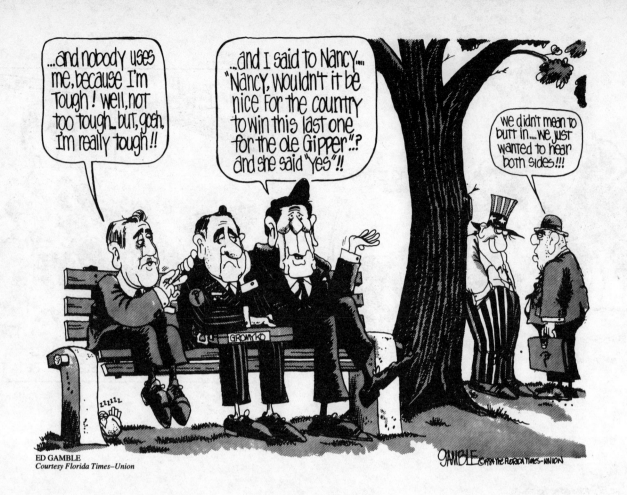

ED GAMBLE
Courtesy Florida Times–Union

JOSEPH HELLER
Courtesy West Bend News (Wisc.)

"IT'S CALLED 'COUNTERBALANCE STRATEGY' COMRADE — FOR EVERY ISRAEL, A SYRIA, FOR EVERY EL SALVADOR, A NICARAGUA... THE AMERICANS SET UP DIPLOMATIC RELATIONS WITH THE VATICAN, SO..."

World Banking

Several large banks in the United States experienced serious financial problems during the year, primarily because of huge foreign loans that were not being repaid on schedule. The world's developing countries, particularly those in Latin America, were staggering under massive debts, and many were unable to make loan payments.

Mexico was the most successful at getting a handle on its financial woes in 1984, instituting stringent austerity measures and persuading banks to lower its interest rate and extend the repayment period. Argentina, facing a foreign debt of $45 billion, declined to institute any meaningful steps to reduce government spending until late in the year. Some budget-cutting was finally made in exchange for $1.4 billion in new credits from the International Monetary Fund.

Chicago's Continental Illinois Corporation, the eighth largest bank holding company in the U.S., almost collapsed during the year. The company had been especially hurt by large loans to energy-related companies that had been purchased from the Penn Square Bank of Oklahoma, which was closed down by federal regulators. A bailout by the Federal Deposit Insurance Corporation was arranged—the largest rescue of any private enterprise in U.S. history.

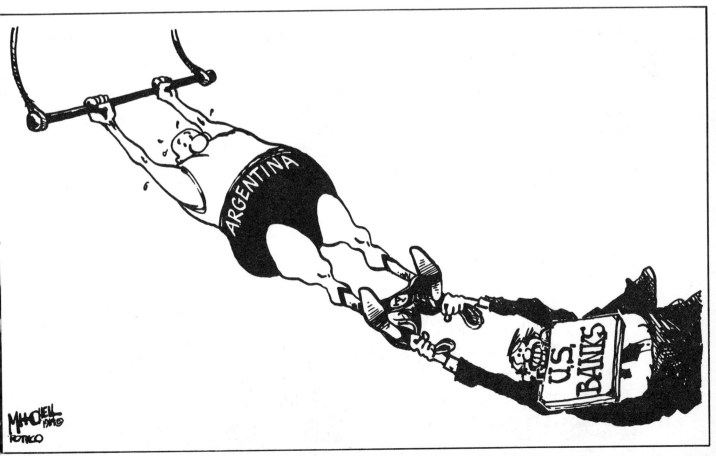

VIC CANTONE
© Rothco

DAN WASSERMAN
© Los Angeles Times Syndicate

GEORGE DANBY
*Courtesy Providence
Journal–Bulletin (R.I.)*

NOT TO WORRY, THE AMBULANCE IS A CHRYSLER

EDDIE GERMANO
Courtesy Brockton Daily Enterprise

The CIA

Ships from six countries, including a Soviet tanker, were damaged by mines in the waters off Nicaragua between March and May of 1984, touching off a heated international debate. At first, the anti-Sandinista Contras claimed responsibility for planting the mines, but news leaks in the U.S. pointed strongly to involvement by the Central Intelligence Agency.

The hand of the CIA was also evident in earlier air strikes and acts of sabotage on pipeline and oil storage facilities in Nicaragua. News of CIA involvement brought cries of outrage from Congress, and the action was condemned by an overwhelming vote. Further military aid to the rebels was cut off by the House of Representatives.

Another furor erupted in Congress and the media in October when it was reported that the CIA had supplied anti-Sandinista rebels with a manual on how to "neutralize" Sandinista officials. This was interpreted to mean that the manual advocated assassination of public officials. A congressional investigation was launched, and President Reagan ordered an inquiry by the CIA's inspector general. The resulting report recommended that several middle-level CIA officials be disciplined.

ETTA HULME
Courtesy Ft. Worth Star–Telegram

OUR MAN IN NICARAGUA

JERRY ROBINSON
© Cartoonists & Writers Syndicate

JERRY BYRD
Courtesy Beaumont Enterprise

CRAIG MACINTOSH
Courtesy Minneapolis Star–Tribune

DENNIS RENAULT
Courtesy Sacramento Bee

'This administration has always been opposed to cowardly acts of international terrorism!'

MIKE SHELTON
Courtesy Orange County Register

"MAY I HAVE YOUR AUTOGRAPH?"

ED ASHLEY
Courtesy Toledo Blade

DICK LOCHER
Courtesy Chicago Tribune

BILL GRAHAM
Courtesy Arkansas Gazette

JOHN TREVER
Courtesy Albuquerque Journal

Space

About thirty spacecraft were launched by the U.S. during the year in a continuing exploration of the heavens. Communications satellites, meteorological satellites, and scientific and technological satellites were placed into orbit, joining those that are still orbiting from previous launches.

The space shuttle *Challenger* lifted off from the Kennedy Space Center in February for the tenth shuttle mission. Two communications satellites were launched from the shuttle, but neither achieved the proper orbit. The eleventh shuttle mission soared into space in April and succeeded in repairing the orbiting Solar Maximum observatory.

The thirteenth shuttle, launched in October, carried a crew of seven, the largest number ever. This trip included two women, Sally K. Ride and Kathryn D. Sullivan, who performed the first spacewalk ever by an American woman. In November, the fourteenth shuttle mission retrieved two expensive satellites that had veered from their programmed orbits, thus proving that practical work in space can be done as problems arise.

President Reagan announced that a schoolteacher would be selected as the first "citizen passenger" to fly in space. The flight will probably take place in late 1985 or 1986.

DOUG MACGREGOR
Courtesy Norwich Bulletin

WAYNE STAYSKAL
Courtesy Tampa Tribune

"MAYBE YOU'D LIKE TO STEP INTO OUTER SPACE AND SAY THAT?"

JOEL PETT
*Courtesy Lexington
Herald–Leader (Ky.)*

LAST SPACE
STATION
for
1,975,000
MILES

ELDON PLETCHER
Courtesy New Orleans Times–Picayune

JIM PALMER
Courtesy Montgomery Advertiser

RALPH DUNAGIN
Courtesy Orlando Sentinel

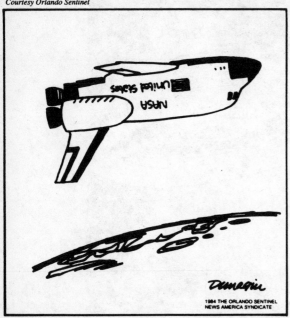

"WAIT A MINUTE...YOU MEAN WE'RE ALL TEACHERS?"

JOHN CRAWFORD
Courtesy Alabama Journal

"SOMETHING'S FINALLY GONNA BE DONE ABOUT THE INCOMPETENT IN OUR CLASSROOMS."

GREAT MOMENTS IN FEAR:
JUST WHEN YOU REALIZE THERE'S *NO SAFE PLACE ON EARTH*, THE ARMS RACE MOVES INTO *SPACE*...

STEVE GREENBERG
Courtesy Los Angeles Daily News

Religion

Religion was a major focal point of the news—and controversy as well—during 1984. In the United States, a great deal of debate centered on the relationship between politics and religion. President Reagan was accused of using religion to aid his reelection campaign through his support for prayer in the schools, and Walter Mondale was accused of injecting religious issues into his campaign as well.

The treatment—or, rather, mistreatment—of Soviet Jews continued to claim world attention. Formal diplomatic relations were established between the U.S. and the Vatican for the first time since 1866. And a black cleric, Bishop Desmond Tutu of South Africa, was awarded the Nobel Peace Prize for speaking out against apartheid in his country.

The Reverend Jesse Jackson, a black minister, quoted Scripture liberally and used religious themes in many of his speeches while campaigning for the Democratic presidential nomination. He drew broad support from black churches throughout the country.

The National Council of Catholic Bishops released a first draft of a proposed pastoral letter concerning the U.S. economy. It focused on the problems of the poor and called for massive changes in government policies to care for their needs. It seemed to regard the profit motive as the cause of poverty and some brand of socialism as the cure.

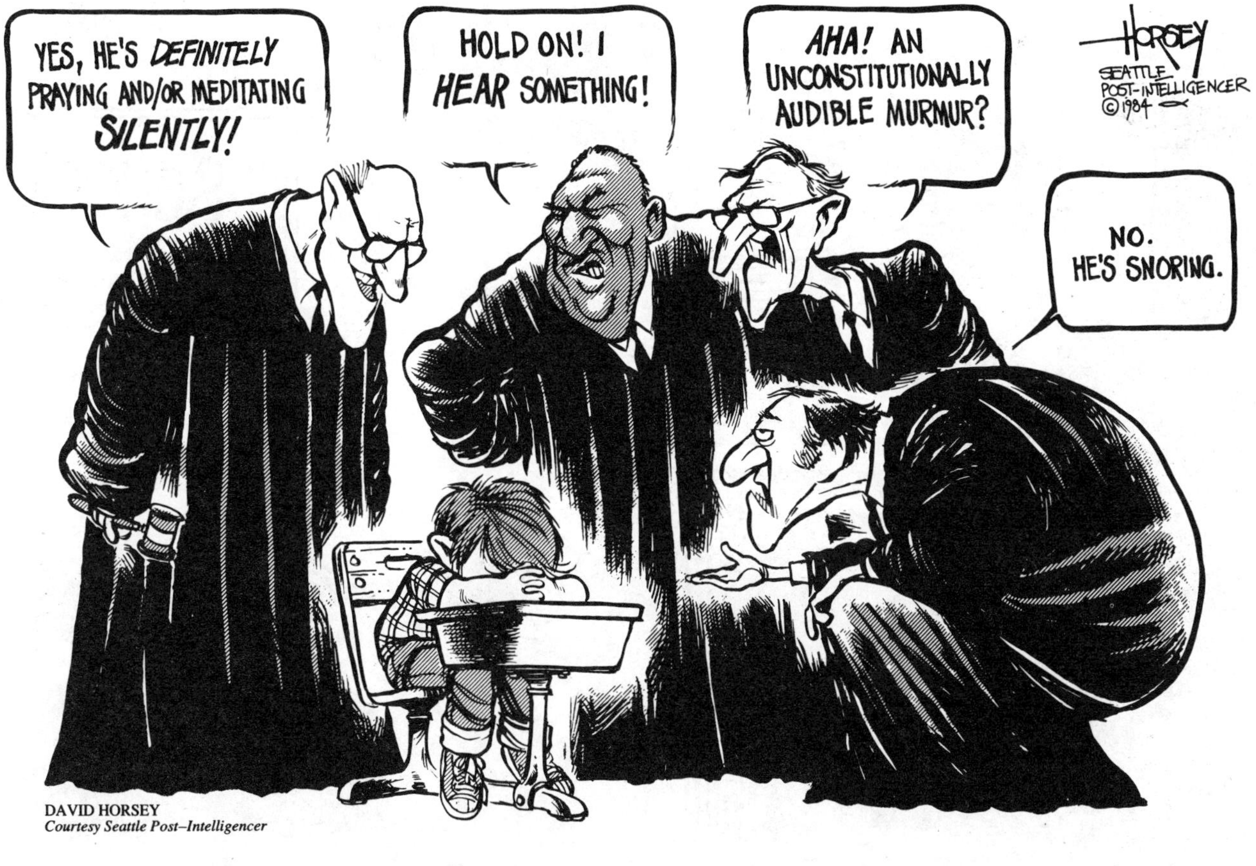
YES, HE'S DEFINITELY PRAYING AND/OR MEDITATING SILENTLY!
HOLD ON! I HEAR SOMETHING!
AHA! AN UNCONSTITUTIONALLY AUDIBLE MURMUR?
NO. HE'S SNORING.
HORSEY
SEATTLE POST-INTELLIGENCER ©1984

DAVID HORSEY
Courtesy Seattle Post–Intelligencer

BOB TAYLOR
Courtesy Dallas Times–Herald

JOHN DEERING
Courtesy Arkansas Democrat

"WILL THAT BE THE PRAYING OR NON-PRAYING SECTION?"

RAY OSRIN
Courtesy Cleveland Plain Dealer

THE 'FATHER' OF HIS COUNTRY.

TOM ENGELHARDT
Courtesy St. Louis Post–Dispatch

'Since The Government Gave Its OK, We're Going
To Hold A Worship Service In Room 215 Today'

JERRY FEARING
*Courtesy St. Paul Dispatch–
Pioneer Press*

CHUCK AYERS
Courtesy Akron Beacon–Journal

"WE CAN STICK IT IN RIGHT ABOUT HERE"

TOM FLANNERY
Courtesy Baltimore Sun

ED GAMBLE
Courtesy Florida Times–Union

Toxic Wastes

The environmental policies of the Reagan administration once again came under attack during 1984. A report prepared for Environmental Safety, a nonpartisan group of professionals in the public health and environmental fields, claimed that only 6 of the 546 highest-priority abandoned toxic waste dumps had been cleaned up since 1980.

After being threatened with legal action, the Environmental Protection Agency agreed in September to reinvestigate possible health dangers from 13 pesticides it had licensed earlier. President Reagan signed legislation in November tightening federal laws concerning toxic waste disposal and extending the laws to cover small companies that had previously been exempt.

Ethylene dibromide, once a major ingredient in 122 pesticide products and believed to cause cancer, was banned as a soil fumigant in 1983. The EPA moved in 1984 to expedite the complete removal of EDB from the U.S. diet.

Acid rain continued in the news, with representatives of 10 nations signing an agreement to reduce industrial emissions of sulfur dioxide by at least 30 percent by 1993. Acid rain may be a contributing factor to downward trends in health and forest growth in the U.S. and Europe, according to the report of a ten-year research study.

CHARLES BISSELL
Courtesy The Tennessean

JIM KNUDSEN
Courtesy L.A. Tidings

GRIM REAPER

RICHARD CROWSON
Courtesy Jackson (Tenn.) Sun

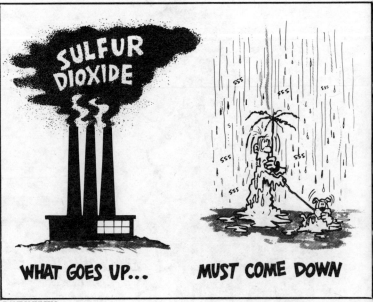

MERLE TINGLEY
Courtesy London Free Press (Can.)

RANDY WICKS
Courtesy Newhall (Calif.) Signal

The Olympics

The 1984 Olympics—both Winter and Summer—were huge successes by any standard. The major winners of the Winter Games, played in Sarajevo, Yugoslavia, were the Soviet Union and East Germany. The Yugoslavs spent some $135 million in preparing the site and hosting the event and, unlike many previous host countries, actually made a profit. The Soviet Union won 25 medals, while East Germany took 24 and Finland captured 13. Norway won 9 and the U.S. and Sweden each won 8. The individual star was Marja-Liisa Hamalainen, a 28-year-old Finnish physiotherapist, who walked off with three gold medals in the women's cross-country races.

The Soviets boycotted the Summer Games in Los Angeles, blaming poor security measures, but the more probable reason was their fear that many of their athletes might take advantage of the opportunity to defect. They were joined in their boycott by more than a dozen of their allies. The XXIII Olympiad proved enormously successful, with capacity crowds viewing the main events in the 93,000 seat Los Angeles Memorial Coliseum. The U.S. won a record 83 gold medals; Romania finished second with 20. The heroes were Carl Lewis, who earned four gold medals in track and field, and gymnasts Li Ning of China and Mary Lou Retton of the U.S. The Games, chaired by Peter Ueberroth, netted a profit of $150 million.

STEVE KELLEY
Courtesy San Diego Union

EDGAR (SOL) SOLLER
Courtesy California Examiner

EDD ULUSCHAK
Courtesy Edmonton Journal

WALT HANDELSMAN
© Patuxent Publishing Corp.

126

MIKE KEEFE
Courtesy Denver Post

DAVID SATTLER
*Courtesy Lafayette (Ind.) Journal and
   Courier*

JIMMY MARGULIES
© Rothco
Courtesy Houston Post

127

DICK WRIGHT
© Scripps-Howard Newspapers

DICK WALLMEYER
Courtesy Independent Press–Telegram
(Calif.)

ART HENRIKSON
© Paddock Publications

Russian Guide to 1984 Summer Games

Soviet Shot Put

Cuban Parallel Bars

Bulgarian Gymnastic Rings

East German Hurdles

Siberian Hammer Throw

Pole Vault

Soviet Diving Team

Soviet Javelin Toss

Soviet Track Team

STEVE BENSON
Courtesy Arizona Republic

BOB ENGLEHART
Courtesy Hartford Courant

JAMES F. TODD
Courtesy Cameron Publications

The Loser...

DAVID HORSEY
Courtesy Seattle Post–Intelligencer

Crime

Several crimes captured the headlines nationwide during 1984, one of the most publicized of which was the trial and ultimate conviction of four men in a shocking barroom gang-rape case. A stream of daily publicity was also given to the trial of automobile magnate John DeLorean, whose discussions with undercover agents in a purported cocaine deal had been videotaped. He was acquitted after a lengthy trial. Some jurors said that DeLorean had been entrapped, while others contended that the government had not proved its case.

In one incident that stunned the nation, an unemployed security guard in San Ysidro, California, allegedly told his wife that he was going "to hunt humans," and then proceeded to a fast-food restaurant and opened fire, killing 21 people and wounding 19 others.

Attention was focused on several cases involving sexual molestation of children. Stories came to light alleging that day-care centers in several states allowed child abuse, and numerous investigations were under way at year's end. Missing children also captured the public's interest, and the National Center for Missing and Exploited Children was established to deal with the problem.

The serious-crime rate dropped for the second consecutive year, perhaps because the national prison population stood at a record 454,136 inmates as of June 1.

— BITTEN AGAIN —

MIKE ANGELO
Courtesy Main Line Times

130

SIGNE WILKINSON
Courtesy San Jose Mercury–News

"OK, YOU HUDDLED MASSES. I KNOW YOU'RE IN HERE."

WAYNE STAYSKAL
Courtesy Tampa Tribune

MIKE MORGAN
Courtesy Macon Telegraph & News

131

TOM DARCY
Courtesy Newsday

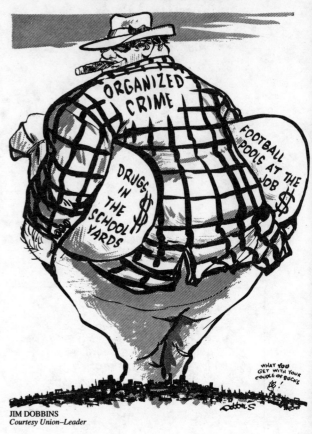

JIM DOBBINS
Courtesy Union–Leader

BILL SANDERS
Courtesy Milwaukee Journal

CHUCK BROOKS
Courtesy Birmingham News

The Courts

Of all the Supreme Court's rulings handed down during the year, one of the most-discussed was the nativity scene case in Pawtucket, Rhode Island. The Court held that a city-sponsored display of the birth of Christ did not violate the establishment clause of the First Amendment which prohibits government from fostering religion.

The Court also ruled that immigration officials may raid businesses suspected of harboring illegal aliens and that states are not required to review death sentences to determine if punishment was "proportional" to similar cases.

In October, Gen. William C. Westmoreland's $120 million libel suit against CBS got under way. Westmoreland, the commander of U.S. forces in Vietnam from 1964 to 1968, contended that a documentary entitled "The Uncounted Enemy: A Vietnam Deception" falsely accused him of having conspired to conceal the true strength of enemy forces from Pres. Lyndon Johnson and other American officials.

Affirmative action proponents were dealt a blow when the Supreme Court ruled that an employer may not be compelled to set aside a valid seniority system in order to protect blacks from layoffs.

In a celebrated case, automobile manufacturer John DeLorean was acquitted in an alleged multi-million-dollar cocaine deal.

WAYNE STAYSKAL
Courtesy Tampa Tribune

"ONE IS HOW MANY DAYS I'VE BEEN HERE. THE OTHER IS MY REPRIEVES. BUT I KEEP FORGETTING WHICH IS WHICH!"

LARRY WRIGHT
Courtesy Detroit News

BEN SARGENT
Courtesy Austin American–Statesman

BILL MITCHELL
© Rothco

TIMOTHY ATSEFF
Courtesy Syracuse Herald–Journal

GENE BASSET
Courtesy Atlanta Journal

Miss America

The staid Miss America Pageant was knocked for a loop during the summer when it was revealed that the reigning Miss America had posed in the nude for a girlie magazine. The September issue of *Penthouse* magazine included photographs of Vanessa Williams, the first black to win the crown, in sexually explicit poses with another woman.

Pageant directors demanded her resignation on grounds that she had violated the contest's standards of moral dignity and wholesomeness. On July 23, Miss Williams relinquished her title, the first Miss America in the history of the Atlantic City pageant to do so. She was succeeded by the runnerup for the title, Suzette Charles, the former Miss New Jersey.

JOHN BRANCH
Courtesy San Antonio Express–News

BILL GARNER
Courtesy Washington Times

LARRY WRIGHT
Courtesy Detroit News

STUART CARLSON
Courtesy Milwaukee Sentinel

The Meese Nomination

President Reagan announced in January that he was nominating presidential counselor Edwin Meese III to replace William French Smith as attorney general. Smith had indicated a wish to return to his law practice in Los Angeles.

The nomination hit a snag in the Senate in March after charges were made that Meese had received financial favors from persons he had assisted in getting government jobs. It was also alleged that he did not testify candidly about his involvement in the theft of Jimmy Carter's debate briefing book when Meese was serving as Reagan's campaign chief of staff in 1980.

A special prosecutor, Jacob Stein of Washington, was named to investigate the charges against Meese. Attorney General Smith agreed to stay on the job until the inquiry was finished. Stein issued a report in September absolving Meese, and the nomination was expected to be approved early in 1985.

ED GAMBLE
Courtesy Florida Times–Union

HUNGER IN NEW ENGLAND?

...The Administration Proclaimeth:

JOHN R. THORNTON
Courtesy Republican Journal

GEORGE FISHER
Courtesy Arkansas Gazette

KEN ALEXANDER
San Francisco Examiner
© Copley News Service

140

Women's Rights

The cause of women's rights scored a breakthrough of sorts in 1984 when Geraldine Ferraro, a New York congresswoman, was nominated by the Democratic Party as its vice-presidential candidate.

The Supreme Court ruled that a state could force the all-male Jaycees organization to admit women as members. Following the ruling, the national leadership of the Jaycees voted overwhelmingly to allow women full membership. The Supreme Court also ruled that law firms are covered by civil rights laws and therefore may not discriminate against women in promoting lawyers to the status of full partner.

The earning power of women in comparison to that of men remained an issue during the year. In late 1983, a case involving the sensitive issue of "comparable worth" cropped up in the state of Washington. A federal judge ruled that the state was violating federal civil rights laws because its salaries for jobs held mostly by women were lower than those for jobs held mostly by men. Washington was ordered to end wage discrimination at once. The ruling cost the state some $400 million in salary adjustments and at year's end was being appealed.

GEORGE FISHER
Courtesy Arkansas Gazette

EARNING POWER
1984

BRIAN GABLE
Courtesy Regina Leader–Post (Sask.)

H. CLAY BENNETT
Courtesy St. Petersburg Times

'OF COURSE I'M AN EQUAL OPPORTUNITY EMPLOYER... I CAN'T
AFFORD TO HIRE A MAN...'

In Memoriam

Indira Gandhi, 66, prime minister of India for 17 of the past 20 years, was assassinated outside her home in New Delhi on October 31, apparently by Sikh members of her personal bodyguard. The daughter of the near-legendary Jawaharlal Nehru, she first became prime minister in 1966.

Russian leader Yuri Vladimirovich Andropov, titular president of the Soviet Union, chairman of the National Defense Council of the U.S.S.R., and general secretary of the Soviet Communist Party, died February 9 in Moscow at the age of 69.

Among other notables who died during the year were: Count Basie, Richard Burton, Rod Cameron, Truman Capote, Frank Church, Gen. Mark Clark, Jackie Coogan, Joe Cronin, William Demarest, Jimmy Demaret, George Gallup, Janet Gaynor, Sam Jaffe, Martin Luther King, Sr., James Mason, Ethel Merman, Slim Pickens, William Powell, Fred Waring, Johnny Weissmuller, and Meredith Willson.

STUART CARLSON
Courtesy Milwaukee Sentinel

HY ROSEN
Courtesy Albany Times–Union

DRAPER HILL
Courtesy Detroit News

ED ASHLEY
Courtesy Toledo Blade

. . . and Other Issues

Amtrak trains seemed to be jinxed during the year, with a series of accidents in July leaving 11 people dead and hundreds injured. In a different kind of disaster, the New Orleans World's Fair closed on November 12 after a six-month run and declared bankruptcy. Estimates of the fair's losses ran as high as $140 million.

The U.S. surgeon general released a new report on the dangers of smoking, citing growing evidence that inhaling smoke from other people's cigarettes can cause health problems.

The Statue of Liberty was enclosed with aluminum scaffolding in July in preparation for extensive structural repairs. Restoration was expected to be completed by 1986, the Lady's 100th birthday.

In October, the heart of a young baboon was transplanted into Baby Fae, an infant suffering from a fatal heart problem. Baby Fae died 20 days later, the longest anyone has ever lived with an animal heart.

In a population conference in Mexico City, the United Nations called upon developing nations to make greater efforts to slow population growth. The U.S. announced it would deny family planning funds to nations that actively promoted or allowed abortions as a means of family planning.

PAUL DUGINSKI
Courtesy Sacramento Bee

JIM ORTON
Courtesy Computerworld

JIM LANGE
Courtesy Daily Oklahoman

MIKE PETERS
Courtesy Dayton Daily News

146

JOHN TREVER
Courtesy Albuquerque Journal

"ODDS ON THE 'OVERLAND FLYER' ARE 4-1, THE 'CAREENING COMET' IS 5-2, AND THE 'LUMBERING LEMMING' IS 7-5...."

JIMMY MARGULIES
Houston Post
© Rothco

WORLD POPULATION CONFERENCE 1984

ETTA ©1984 FORT WORTH STAR-TELEGRAM
HULME
NEA

FERTILITY GODS

USA

FAMILY PLANNING   FAMILY PLANNING   FAMILY PLANNING   FAMILY PLANNING

MEXICO   EUROPE   INDIA   CHINA, ETC

ETTA HULME
Courtesy Ft. Worth Star–Telegram

JIMMY MARGULIES
Houston Post
© Rothco

MARGULIES
©1984 HOUSTON POST

WORLD POPULATION
CONFERENCE

FAMILY PLANNING LITERATURE   CONTRACEPTIVE SAMPLES   BIRTH CONTROL COUNSELING   CIGARS

JIM ORTON
Courtesy Computerworld

MARTIN E. GARRITY
Courtesy Fair Oaks Post (Calif.)

ART HENRIKSON
© Paddock Publications

JACK HIGGINS
Courtesy Chicago Sun–Times

TOM ADDISON
Courtesy The Journal (S.C.)

JOHN CRAWFORD
Courtesy Alabama Journal

STEVE LINDSTROM
Courtesy Duluth News–Tribune

JERRY BARNETT
Courtesy Indianapolis News

JIM DOBBINS
Courtesy Union–Leader

151

EDD ULUSCHAK
Courtesy Edmonton Journal

"Sorry, it was a reflex action — I'm with the Parole Board."

BLAINE
Courtesy The Spectator (Ont.)

CHUCK ASAY
Courtesy Colorado Springs Sun

BRUCE BEATTIE
*Courtesy Daytona Beach
News–Journal*

GREG KEARNEY
Courtesy Casper Star–Tribune (Wyom.)

"We have a new landmark since we started our experiments with capitalism...
It's the Great Mall of China..."

STEVE SACK
Courtesy Minneapolis Tribune

DAVID HORSEY
Courtesy Seattle Post–Intelligencer

JERRY BARNETT
Courtesy Indianapolis News

LAZARO FRESQUET
Courtesy El Miami Herald

VIC CANTONE
Courtesy New York Daily News

THE SKY'S THE LIMIT

V. CULLUM ROGERS
Courtesy Durham Morning Herald

PETER B. WALLACE
Courtesy Boston Herald

Past Award Winners

PULITZER PRIZE EDITORIAL CARTOON

1922—Rollin Kirby, New York World
1924—J. N. Darling, New York Herald Tribune
1925—Rollin Kirby, New York World
1926—D. R. Fitzpatrick, St. Louis Post-Dispatch
1927—Nelson Harding, Brooklyn Eagle
1928—Nelson Harding, Brooklyn Eagle
1929—Rollin Kirby, New York World
1930—Charles Macauley, Brooklyn Eagle
1931—Edmund Duffy, Baltimore Sun
1932—John T. McCutcheon, Chicago Tribune
1933—H. M. Talburt, Washington Daily News
1934—Edmund Duffy, Baltimore Sun
1935—Ross A. Lewis, Milwaukee Journal
1937—C. D. Batchelor, New York Daily News
1938—Vaughn Shoemaker, Chicago Daily News
1939—Charles G. Werner, Daily Oklahoman
1940—Edmund Duffy, Baltimore Sun
1941—Jacob Burck, Chicago Times
1942—Herbert L. Block, Newspaper Enterprise Association
1943—Jay N. Darling, New York Herald Tribune
1944—Clifford K. Berryman, Washington Star
1945—Bill Mauldin, United Feature Syndicate
1946—Bruce Russell, Los Angeles Times
1947—Vaughn Shoemaker, Chicago Daily News
1948—Reuben L. (Rube) Goldberg, New York Sun
1949—Lute Pease, Newark Evening News
1950—James T. Berryman, Washington Star
1951—Reginald W. Manning, Arizona Republic
1952—Fred L. Packer, New York Mirror
1953—Edward D. Kuekes, Cleveland Plain Dealer
1954—Herbert L. Block, Washington Post
1955—Daniel R. Fitzpatrick, St. Louis Post-Dispatch
1956—Robert York, Louisville Times
1957—Tom Little, Nashville Tennessean
1958—Bruce M. Shanks, Buffalo Evening News
1959—Bill Mauldin, St. Louis Post-Dispatch
1961—Carey Orr, Chicago Tribune
1962—Edmund S. Valtman, Hartford Times
1963—Frank Miller, Des Moines Register
1964—Paul Conrad, Denver Post
1966—Don Wright, Miami News
1967—Patrick B. Oliphant, Denver Post
1968—Eugene Gray Payne, Charlotte Observer
1969—John Fischetti, Chicago Daily News
1970—Thomas F. Darcy, Newsday
1971—Paul Conrad, Los Angeles Times
1972—Jeffrey K. MacNelly, Richmond News Leader
1974—Paul Szep, Boston Globe
1975—Garry Trudeau, Universal Press Syndicate
1976—Tony Auth, Philadelphia Enquirer
1977—Paul Szep, Boston Globe
1978—Jeff MacNelly, Richmond News Leader
1979—Herbert Block, Washington Post
1980—Don Wright, Miami News
1981—Mike Peters, Dayton Daily News
1982—Ben Sargent, Austin American-Statesman
1983—Dick Locher, Chicago Tribune
1984—Paul Conrad, Los Angeles Times

NOTE: Pulitzer Prize Award was not given 1923, 1936, 1960, 1965, and 1973.

SIGMA DELTA CHI EDITORIAL CARTOON

1942—Jacob Burck, Chicago Times
1943—Charles Werner, Chicago Sun
1944—Henry Barrow, Associated Press
1945—Reuben L. Goldberg, New York Sun
1946—Dorman H. Smith, Newspaper Enterprise Association
1947—Bruce Russell, Los Angeles Times
1948—Herbert Block, Washington Post
1949—Herbert Block, Washington Post
1950—Bruce Russell, Los Angeles Times
1951—Herbert Block, Washington Post, and Bruce Russell, Los Angeles Times
1952—Cecil Jensen, Chicago Daily News
1953—John Fischetti, Newspaper Enterprise Association
1954—Calvin Alley, Memphis Commercial Appeal
1955—John Fischetti, Newspaper Enterprise Association
1956—Herbert Block, Washington Post
1957—Scott Long, Minneapolis Tribune
1958—Clifford H. Baldowski, Atlanta Constitution
1959—Charles G. Brooks, Birmingham News
1960—Dan Dowling, New York Herald-Tribune
1961—Frank Interlandi, Des Moines Register
1962—Paul Conrad, Denver Post
1963—William Mauldin, Chicago Sun-Times
1964—Charles Bissell, Nashville Tennessean
1965—Roy Justus, Minneapolis Star
1966—Patrick Oliphant, Denver Post
1967—Eugene Payne, Charlotte Observer
1968—Paul Conrad, Los Angeles Times
1969—William Mauldin, Chicago Sun-Times
1970—Paul Conrad, Los Angeles Times
1971—Hugh Haynie, Louisville Courier-Journal
1972—William Mauldin, Chicago Sun-Times
1973—Paul Szep, Boston Globe
1974—Mike Peters, Dayton Daily News
1975—Tony Auth, Philadelphia Enquirer
1976—Paul Szep, Boston Globe
1977—Don Wright, Miami News
1978—Jim Borgman, Cincinnati Enquirer
1979—John P. Trever, Albuquerque Journal
1980—Paul Conrad, Los Angeles Times
1981—Paul Conrad, Los Angeles Times
1982—Dick Locher, Chicago Tribune
1983—Rob Lawlor, Philadelphia Daily News

NATIONAL HEADLINERS CLUB AWARD EDITORIAL CARTOON

1938—C. D. Batchelor, New York Daily News
1939—John Knott, Dallas News
1940—Herbert Block, Newspaper Enterprise Association
1941—Charles H. Sykes, Philadelphia Evening Ledger
1942—Jerry Doyle, Philadelphia Record
1943—Vaughn Shoemaker, Chicago Daily News
1944—Roy Justus, Sioux City Journal
1945—F. O. Alexander, Philadelphia Bulletin
1946—Hank Barrow, Associated Press
1947—Cy Hungerford, Pittsburgh Post-Gazette
1948—Tom Little, Nashville Tennessean
1949—Bruce Russell, Los Angeles Times
1950—Dorman Smith, Newspaper Enterprise Association
1951—C. G. Werner, Indianapolis Star
1952—John Fischetti, Newspaper Enterprise Association
1953—James T. Berryman and Gib Crockett, Washington Star
1954—Scott Long, Minneapolis Tribune
1955—Leo Thiele, Los Angeles Mirror-News
1956—John Milt Morris, Associated Press
1957—Frank Miller, Des Moines Register
1958—Burris Jenkins, Jr., New York Journal-American
1959—Karl Hubenthal, Los Angeles Examiner
1960—Don Hesse, St. Louis Globe-Democrat
1961—L. D. Warren, Cincinnati Enquirer
1962—Franklin Morse, Los Angeles Mirror
1963—Charles Bissell, Nashville Tennessean
1964—Lou Grant, Oakland Tribune
1965—Merle R. Tingley, London (Ont.) Free Press
1966—Hugh Haynie, Louisville Courier-Journal
1967—Jim Berry, Newspaper Enterprise Association
1968—Warren King, New York News
1969—Larry Barton, Toledo Blade
1970—Bill Crawford, Newspaper Enterprise Association
1971—Ray Osrin, Cleveland Plain Dealer
1972—Jacob Burck, Chicago Sun-Times
1973—Ranan Lurie, New York Times
1974—Tom Darcy, Newsday
1975—Bill Sanders, Milwaukee Journal
1976—No award given
1977—Paul Szep, Boston Globe
1978—Dwane Powell, Raleigh News and Observer
1979—Pat Oliphant, Washington Star
1980—Don Wright, Miami News
1981—Bill Garner, Memphis Commercial Appeal
1982—Mike Peters, Dayton Daily News
1983—Doug Marlette, Charlotte Observer
1984—Steve Benson, Arizona Republic

NATIONAL NEWSPAPER AWARD/CANADA EDITORIAL CARTOON

1949—Jack Boothe, Toronto Globe and Mail
1950—James G. Reidford, Montreal Star
1951—Len Norris, Vancouver Sun
1952—Robert La Palme, Le Devoir, Montreal
1953—Robert W. Chambers, Halifax Chronicle-Herald
1954—John Collins, Montreal Gazette
1955—Merle R. Tingley, London Free Press
1956—James G. Reidford, Toronto Globe and Mail
1957—James G. Reidford, Toronto Globe and Mail
1958—Raoul Hunter, Le Soleil, Quebec
1959—Duncan Macpherson, Toronto Star
1960—Duncan Macpherson, Toronto Star
1961—Ed McNally, Montreal Star
1962—Duncan Macpherson, Toronto Star
1963—Jan Kamienski, Winnipeg Tribune
1964—Ed McNally, Montreal Star
1965—Duncan Macpherson, Toronto Star
1966—Robert W. Chambers, Halifax Chronicle-Herald
1967—Raoul Hunter, Le Soleil, Quebec
1968—Roy Peterson, Vancouver Sun
1969—Edward Uluschak, Edmonton Journal
1970—Duncan Macpherson, Toronto Daily Star
1971—Yardley Jones, Toronto Sun
1972—Duncan Macpherson, Toronto Star
1973—John Collins, Montreal Gazette
1974—Blaine, Hamilton Spectator
1975—Roy Peterson, Vancouver Sun
1976—Andy Donato, Toronto Sun
1977—Terry Mosher, Montreal Gazette
1978—Terry Mosher, Montreal Gazette
1979—Edd Uluschak, Edmonton Journal
1980—Vic Roschkov, Toronto Star
1981—Tom Innes, Calgary Herald
1982—Blaine, Hamilton Spectator
1983—Dale Cummings, Winnipeg Free Press

OVERSEAS PRESS CLUB AWARD EDITORIAL CARTOON

1971—Tom Darcy, Newsday
1972—Don Wright, Miami News
1973—Tom Darcy, Newsday
1974—Warren King, New York Daily News
1975—Tony Auth, Philadelphia Inquirer
1976—Tony Auth, Philadelphia Inquirer
1977—Warren King, New York Daily News
1978—Ed Fischer, Omaha World-Herald
1979—Jim Morin, Miami Herald
1980—Don Wright, Miami News
1981—Paul Conrad, Los Angeles Times
1982—Don Wright, Miami News
1983—Dick Locher, Chicago Tribune
1984—Dick Locher, Chicago Tribune

Index

INDEX